EDMUND SPENSER

*from a portrait at Pembroke College, Cambridge,
reproduced by kind permission of the Master and Fellows*

EDMUND SPENSER

by
ALASTAIR FOWLER

Edited by Ian Scott-Kilvert

PUBLISHED FOR
THE BRITISH COUNCIL
BY LONGMAN GROUP LTD

LONGMAN GROUP LTD
Longman House, Burnt Mill, Harlow, Essex

*Associated companies, branches and
representatives throughout the world*

First published 1977
© Alastair Fowler 1977

*Printed in England by
Bradleys, Reading and London*

ISBN 0 582 01271 6

EDMUND SPENSER

I

'Sage Homer, Virgil, Spenser laureate'. Spenser is one of our few classics. For that very reason, although his status has never been very seriously threatened, ideas of him have changed. Different ages and critics have given very different accounts of his work. Up to the eighteenth century, his reputation depended far more than it would now on *The Shepherd's Calendar*. Spenser was consequently a pastoral and love poet: even in *The Faerie Queen* he was 'Heroic Paramour of Faerie Land', to be compared with Ariosto or Petrarch. On the other hand he was also a learned poet, English Virgil, edited, cited as an *auctor* and widely imitated. This posed problems for neoclassically minded readers, who had a blindingly clear idea of exactly what a classic work ought to be. *The Faerie Queen* could easily seem a bit too 'uncultivate' and Gothic. Their solution was to turn attention away from Spenser's design, which broke too many rules, to the serious moral content—or else to his descriptive pictorial art. *The Faerie Queen* became 'an excellent piece of morality, policy, history'—or Mrs Spence's 'gallery of pictures'. The influential Hughes completed this development by combining both approaches. He showed how Spenser could be valued both as an 'imager of virtues and vices' and a 'rough painter' ('The embellishments of description are rich and lavish in him beyond comparison'), without looking to him for epic or romance coherence.

Unfortunately Spenser's morality was largely embodied in allegory. If the neoclassical critics were prepared to accord this element a lowly but secure place, 'allegories fulsome grow', and the Romantic critics were inclined to jettison it altogether. For Hazlitt the allegory was something that would not bite so long as you left it alone. Even the perceptive critic James Russell Lowell followed this approach, recommending *The Faerie Queen* to those who wished 'to be rid of thought'. Spenser's sensuous vividness has always remained, together perhaps with the dazzling ease of transitions, and a deeper, more elusive imaginativeness, closer to dream. However variously described and subject to misunderstanding, he has occupied a special place in our literature, as a nourisher of other poets' work. He was Cowley's first introduction to poetry; Pope's 'mistress'; Wordsworth's 'inspiration'; and a model to Milton, Dryden, Thomson, Yeats and countless others. By almost common consent he is one of our most 'poetic' poets, so that he serves as a sounding board even for those of a very different temper: his words run softly even through the lines of an Eliot.

Twentieth-century criticism has been better equipped historically to interpret the poetry that Spenser wrote. Sharing a common view of him as a great and serious poet, it has mostly been taken up with explaining. The explanation tends to be detailed: the picture gallery has given way to iconographical studies. Our best modern criticism is technically remarkable; but it usually lacks the proportion achieved in the eighteenth century by John Upton, still Spenser's best reader. Perhaps in consequence some judicial critics, who would not quite deny the greatness of Spenser, have nevertheless thought his poetry too much in need of difficult explanation to be worth the effort for modern readers. They have renewed and reinforced Jonson's objections to his poetic diction and the Augustan charges of structural faults; or fallen back on the position that 'the wittiest poets have been all short' (Felltham). Neocritical, in fact, is neoclassical writ small. Recently, however, critics have shown more interest in longer poems. At the same time, a better appreciation of Gothic interlace—interweaving of linear narratives—is allowing revaluation of Spenser's complex neo-Gothic form. Very early on, Hughes and Hurd guessed that Spenser's Gothic cathedral might have its own kind of unity. But the implications of that valuable analogy can only now be fully developed. Poetry such as Spenser's is too central to our literature to be really threatened by critical opinion: some of it is too profound even to need much conscious understanding. Still, it is as well, from time to time, to revise our notion of the achievement. Where are Spenser's excellences, for us? We are beginning to have more interest than our predecessors in his vision of the totality of human experience: a vision as wide, in its way, as Milton's or Blake's or MacDiarmid's. We should be more inclined to see him as pursuing the highest and most philosophical ends of poetry.

II

Not much is known about Spenser's life. He was born in London, his 'most kindly nurse', probably in 1552. Although related to the noble Spencers of Warwickshire and Northamptonshire, his immediate family circumstances seem to have been poor. He was educated at Merchant Taylors' School, an outstanding new grammar school, which he attended for eight years from its foundation in 1561. There the curriculum included a great deal of Latin, some Greek (certainly Homer), and the Hebrew psalter. As in other grammar schools, the Latin would be not only classical but Renaissance: Erasmus, Vives, perhaps Mantuanus's pastorals or Palingenius's *Zodiacus vitae*. Exceptionally, the curriculum extended to music, and possibly even to English. For the headmaster was an advanced educationalist, the great Richard Mulcaster. No doctrinaire Humanist, Mulcaster had a strong and original mind, which he expressed in a fine though sometimes obscure style. The ideas developed in *Positions* and *The Elementary* are sometimes ahead of any that have even yet been realized; nevertheless, they are compatible with a deep sense of history. The latter gave Mulcaster a reverence for such fragile institutions as customs and languages. Thus, his classicism allowed for the possibility of different classical periods in modern literatures. He read Ariosto; he advocated regular teaching of the vernacular ('I honour Latin, but worship English'); he defended the education of women. Many of Mulcaster's ideas seem to find a later echo in Spenser's writing: not least the belief that literature and learning may form the character of the individual for the public good.

Together with Lancelot Andrewes, Spenser left school in 1569 for Pembroke Hall, Cambridge, where he was a sizar, paying no fees but performing certain chores. The next four years were spent in completing the trivium begun at school, by reading rhetoric, logic and philosophy; the three years after on the quadrivium, arithmetic, geometry, astronomy and music. These studies centred on a small number of set authors, all classical. In 1573 Spenser proceeded B.A.; in 1576 M.A. At Cambridge an oral tradition then vigorously prevailed, of lectures and public disputation. The level of learned eloquence was high, fitting an excessive number for the administrative offices available. (The size of the university was nevertheless small by modern standards: about 1,800 of whom 250 were sizars.) Spenser's contempories included the much older Thomas Preston, author of *Cambyses;* the younger Abraham Fraunce, poet, rhetorician, literary theorist; and Gabriel Harvey.

Harvey, who was Spenser's senior by about three years, became a Fellow of Pembroke Hall in 1570, Praelector (or Professor) of Rhetoric in 1574. His *Ciceronianus* and *Rhetor* show him to have been a brilliant scholar and writer; surely one of the sharpest minds of his time. And he was probably, as Virginia Woolf surmized, a brilliant talker. Yet his Cambridge career was erratic, and in the end unsuccessful. This may have been not altogether to his discredit; he had ideas progressive enough to provoke opposition—including Ramist reform in logic, and unsound 'paradoxes' such as Copernicus's heliocentric hypothesis. But he was also arrogant, quarrelsome, tactless, vain, silly, and a misfit. The man who could write 'Sometime my book is unto me a god/ Sometime I throw it from me a rod' was too restless for mere scholarship. In another age he might have been a literary critic, or even a columnist. As it was, he went after preferment with the desperation of frustrated greatness, perpetually encouraging himself the while, in countless Macchiavellian marginalia, to futile circumspections.

In spite (or perhaps because) of our knowing so many of his private thoughts, he remains a baffling figure. Most—like Nashe in their public quarrel, and perhaps Shakespeare, in Holofernes—have regarded him as a foolish pedant. He took himself seriously; so that others have tended not to. But it is not Harvey who seems pedantic when Spenser and he differ about quantity in English verse. His greater experience and wide reading enabled him to enlarge Spenser's tastes, and perhaps to make him more contemporary, more European. He came to recognize the quality of an early version of *The Faerie Queen*; although he preferred (rightly or wrongly) Spenser's lost *Comedies*. But this advice was resisted. Spenser was well able to exert his own taste decisively; using a bet, for example, to press Harvey to read *Lazarillo de Tormes*. Their friendship, which mattered to both men, was reciprocal and not dependent. How did Spenser regard him? The sonnet he addressed to Harvey from Dublin in 1586 seems comically inappropriate now: 'happy above happiest men ... sitting like a looker-on/Of this world's stage', wielding his 'critic pen', careless of suspicion. But Harvey, who was not yet the failure of later years, nor demeaned by controversy with the unfair and clever Nashe, perhaps had still an outsider's early idealism. However that may be, this strange man also cherished ambitious hopes of following in the footsteps of Cheke and Smith, and of becoming great in the councils of the mighty. From 1576 he pursued the favour of Leicester, and from 1578 of Sidney. He was thus in a position to introduce Spenser to two of the greatest patrons of the age. And when Spenser's *Shepherd's Calendar* appeared anonymously in 1579, it bore a dedication to Sidney.

Although the Cambridge of Spenser's day was dominated by radical Puritans of Thomas Cartwright's stamp, Spenser emerged a moderate but fervent Protestant, with views comparable to those of Richard Hooker or gentle Archbishop Grindal (the Algrin of *The Shepherd's Calendar*). In 1578, after some time in the north, he became secretary to Edward Young, the former Master of Pembroke Hall. By 5 October in the year following, however, he had entered the household of the Earl of Leicester, and was familiar with Leicester's nephew Sir Philip Sidney. Together with Sidney and Sir Edward Dyer he made the experiments in 'artificial' or quantitative verse that are discussed and developed in the correspondence with Harvey, published in 1580 as *Three proper, and witty, familiar Letters*. (This spirited but unsuccessful attempt to capture in the vernacular the sophisticated obliquity of smart neo-Latin epistles got Gabriel Harvey into a great deal of trouble with the authorities.) Probably about the same time, Spenser was writing his 'lost' works (*Epithalamion Thamesis, The Court of Cupid, Dreams, Pageants*, etc.), some of which may be early versions of parts of *The Faerie Queen*. Also in 1579 he married, almost certainly, Machabyas Childe, by whom he was to have two children, Sylvanus and Katherine.

Then, in 1580, Spenser went to Ireland as Secretary to the new Governor, Arthur Lord Grey. (The English were making another of their incoherent attempts to Anglicize barbarous Ireland, partly by colonial settlement, partly by the sword.) Inexplicably this move has been represented as exile consequent on some disgrace (perhaps Spenser offended Leicester, as *Virgil's Gnat* hints?) But humanistically trained men of letters expected and hoped to exercise their pens in administrative tasks. A career's success was gauged by the minor offices collected, and the estates. Spenser was Clerk of Faculties in the Court of Chancery (1581: a sinecure); Commissioner for Musters (1583); Deputy to Lodowick Bryskett as Clerk of the Council of Munster (1584); Prebendary of Limerick Cathedral (1585: a sinecure); and Justice of the County of Cork (1594). From 1582 he leased New Abbey near Dublin; in 1586 he was assigned, and in 1590 formally granted, the very large estate of Kilcolman (3,000 acres, or about 1,214 hectares). Kilcolman was Spenser's real and emotional home: its landscape finds reflection in many passages of his poetry. In fact, he should be regarded as one of our great Irish writers.

Even in Ireland, however, he still belonged to the literary milieu of the court. Lodowick Bryskett, whose dialogue *Discourse of Civil Life* (1583) has Spenser as one of its interlocutors, was a poet and former tutor of Sidney's. Raleigh visited his nearby estate in 1589. And manuscript circulation of Spenser's work is argued by Abraham Fraunce's ability to quote from *The Faerie Queen* Book 2 before its publication. In 1589 and again in 1595 or 1596 Spenser made visits to London that occasioned flurries of publication, partly of old work revised: 1590, *The Faerie Queen*, Part 1 and *Muiopotmos*; 1591, *Daphnaida* and *Complaints*; 1595, *Amoretti and Epithalamion* and *Colin Clout's Come Home*

Again; 1596, *The Faerie Queen,* Part 2, *Prothalamion* and the *Hymns. The Faerie Queen* may never have been finished. Of the six missing books, only the Cantos of Mutability (published posthumously) remain.

The *Complaints* volume was suppressed, probably because Spenser had criticized Lord Burleigh in *The Ruins of Time* and *Mother Hubberd's Tale.* Burleigh was nevertheless included, though cautiously, among the sixteen nobles to whom *The Faerie Queen* was presented: it was dedicated to the Queen herself. He seems not to have liked it. The Queen, however, did. She paid Spenser the unique honour in 1591 of a life pension, £50 p.a. (a considerable sum: more than twice the rent for Kilcolman). In 1594 Spenser was remarried, to Elizabeth Boyle. He solemnized the wedding day, June 11, in *Amoretti and Epithalamion.* 1596 finds him celebrating with *Prothalamion* the spousals of the Earl of Worcester's daughters at Essex House in London. The poem expresses 'old woes', the loss of his patron Leicester, who died in 1588, and his consequent friendlessness; but it also looks forward to the favour of a new patron, the Earl of Essex. Spenser's successful career culminated with his nomination (as one 'with good knowledge in learning and not unskilful or without experience in the service of the wars') to the post of High Sheriff of Cork, on 30 September 1598. But within a month the rebels had overrun Munster and burnt Kilcolman. Spenser returned to London with dispatches on Christmas Eve; and on 13 January 1599 he died. He was buried in Westminster Abbey, near to Chaucer, at the expense of Essex, 'his hearse being carried by poets, and mournful verses and poems thrown into his tomb'. There was an early tradition that Spenser died in want; but it seems to have been without basis.

III

The Shepherd's Calendar (1579) was Spenser's first considerable published work. This fact is a little misleading, in that he already had behind him the lost works, not to speak of the schoolboy translation of Van der Noodt's Protestant emblem book. Spenser was early drawn to poetry, yet had a slow development as a poet. Traditionally, pastoral offered an unassuming mode that might be attempted in prelude to more ambitious flights. *The Shepherd's Calendar*, however, is far from being apprentice work. It shows a high sense of control, and yet an astonishing freedom in the treatment of genre. It is far from mere imitation or combination of Theocritus, Virgil, Mantuan and Marot. Indeed, considered historically, its achievement is so considerable as to make it a watershed on any map of English verse.

Spenser enlarged the pastoral tradition in several ways. Renaissance eclogues by Mantuan and Barclay had already treated moral or religious matters: pastoral could be microcosmic and satiric rather than idyllic. Spenser took up this option and invested in it heavily. The landscape that he makes a mirror of his shepherd's plight is 'barren ground, whom winter's wrath hath wasted': a land suffering from adverse weather, wolves and disease. In fact, it is real country. And he introduces many fresh images from nature (such as the oak's top 'bald and wasted with worms' or the bee 'working her formal rooms in waxen frame'), besides many country phrases not previously heard in serious poetry.

Most creative of all is his approach to the structure. Instead of the usual collection of independent 'eclogues' (the term anciently implied separateness), Spenser has made a single work, unified by the structural principle of the natural year, and of seasons that symbolize stages in human life. As Pope noted, 'the addition he has made of a calendar to his eclogues is very beautiful'. The calendrical form not only holds the eclogues together, but contributes to their special character of endless variety combined with complex, elusive order. It works multifariously: in the changing weather; in seasonal customs (April's flower gathering was the occupation for that month by the conventions of visual art); explicitly astronomical imagery (Sol appears in July, the month of his own sign Leo, 'making his way between the Cup,/and golden Diadem'); and even in physical proportions (May is by far the longest eclogue, since the sun was known to stay longer in Gemini than in any other sign).

Spenser also achieved controlled variety by varying the metre, all the way from rough alliterative lines to the gentle, grave stateliness of November's elegy for Dido:

> But now sike [such] happy cheer is turned to heavy chance,
>   Such pleasance now displaced by dolour's dint:
> All music sleeps, where death doth lead the dance,
>   And shepherds' wonted solace is extinct.
> The blue in black, the green in grey is tinct [tinged],
>   The gaudy garlands deck her grave,
>   The faded flowers her corse embrave.
>   O heavy hearse,
> Mourn now my Muse, now mourn with tears besprint
>   [sprinkled].
>   O careful verse.
>
>   (November, 103-12)

Inset songs and fables introduce farther variation. Then there is the alternation of three modes or categories ('plaintive', 'moral' and 'recreative'); and the interweaving of three large subjects: love, poetry, and religious politics. The command with which genres are deployed makes for admiration, even where this is not accompanied with understanding or enjoyment. Everything seems in scale, and orchestrated; giving a sense of various modes of life in harmony. January's love complaint gives way to February's *débat* between youth and age, which encloses (and perhaps underlies too) the fable of an episcopal oak and a Puritan briar. March offers an exploit of Cupid; April, an inset ode in praise of Elizabeth, with some delicately Skeltonic flower poetry; and May, a beast fable and more controversy.

The poetic statement made on this complex instrument is itself complex. For one thing, the shepherds enact a *roman-à-clef*, to which the key has been lost. Algrin is Grindal and Hobbinol Gabriel Harvey; but others remain unidentified, even with the help of fashionably elaborate annotation by 'E.K.' (himself unknown). Moreover, some of the roles are multivalent. Thus, besides being a *persona* for Spenser, Colin Clout is a highly idealized laureate (combining poetic names from Skelton and Marot). Tityrus is both Virgil and Chaucer. And Pan figures severally as Henry VIII, as the Pope, and as

Christ. Nevertheless, the topical allegory is probably not intricate: Spenser seems to have tended to political simplicity as much as to intellectual subtlety.

Nowhere is there more subtlety than in the poem's structural pattern. To begin with, it sets out two calendars: the astronomical, running from March to February, and the Christian, from January to December. Circularity is suggested by the linking of the January and December eclogues, which have each the single speaker Colin. They are 'proportionable' in the octave ratio of perfect harmony, one being exactly twice as long as the other. Then, the plaintive, moral and recreative eclogues are arranged, with their speakers, in interlocking symmetries. For example, January to June (corresponding astrologically to the six 'lunar' signs) form the sequence $p/m/r/r/m/p$. Moreover, Colin's concluding motto in June, as E.K. notes, answers that in January. Thus, the first half of the *Calendar* also forms a circle, a subsidiary 'world', which may be interpreted as the mundane world of natural life. It begins with Colin's 'wilfully' breaking his pipe, and ends with his giving up false love and the unworthy Rosalind. Within this world are conflicts between the old and the new (February: oak *vs.* briar), or between worldly pleasure and censorious morality (May: Palinode *vs.* Piers). June, however, makes the challenges to an earthly paradise explicit; leading to July's myth of the Fall, and fatal disorders in nature. Here, at the poem's centre, stands a mountain, the high place of God: there is mention of Sinai, Olivet and 'mighty Pan' or Christ.

The *Calendar*'s second half becomes increasingly dark, the secular idyll more and more plainly illusion. Art's solace now replaces that of nature. But the mirror of art, which itself mirrors nature, brings deeper disenchantments still. October questions the use of poetry and even the possibility of literary life. Its talk of war contradicts the olive coronal of April, the matching month (with sign in opposition) of the *Calendar*'s first half. To lighten this gloom there emerges the theme of grace. In September Diggon Davie repents, in December Colin himself. Indeed, one might see the whole *Calendar* as a confession of Colin's developing religious consciousness: as his palinode or retraction from earlier secularity. But the poem is more inclusive, more Chaucerian perhaps, than this would suggest. It finds room, after all, for natural beauty, for the worldly Palinode, for the retired Hobbinol. And it is the reformer Piers who overstates his case. The *Calendar* leaves us, in the end, with a sense of manifold fictive worlds, all comprehended in Spenser's detached vision of mutability.

This marvellous intellectual structure unfortunately no longer quite succeeds as poetry. This is not merely because of its coterie aspects—these are no insuperable obstacle with Shakespeare's poems. The reasons have to do with certain critical theories, fashionable in Spenser's day, about the language of literature. Following ideas of Du Bellay and others, he believed that a classical English style could be based on Chaucer's language. Hence his interweaving of rustic expressions appropriate to pastoral, Chaucerian archaisms and ancient poetic words ('grieslie', 'moe', 'astert'), together with contrastingly easy conventional epithets ('riper age', 'doleful verse'), to form a lexical tapestry of great, perhaps even excessive, richness. Specially desirable were dialectal or pseudodialectal words, parts, or mere spelling variants that preserved Chaucer's, Gavin Douglas's and earlier forms ('swincke'; 'sayne'). This diction was not quite so experimental then as it has since come to look; but intensified as it was by archaistic syntax and combined with a style of plain pithy statement, its effect must always have been singular enough. Jonson says that Spenser 'writ no language'. Spenser might appeal to Theocritus's precedent— and to the many poets who have followed his rather than Jonson's example. The smooth element of Spenser's diction has influenced poetic taste ever since. But some of his rougher innovations now seem as decisively wrong-headed as any in Wordsworth's *Lyrical Ballads*:

> My ragged ronts [bullocks] all shiver and shake,
> As doen high towers in an earthquake. . . .

> (February 5–6)

Another unfortunate theory concerned Chaucer's versification. At a time when the Chaucerian canon was uncertain, and accessible only in bad texts, his verse was universally held to be rough. It was imitated by such devices as the addition of final -e. Spenser's fashionably rough verse now seems almost as dated as that of his contemporaries. At best it is workmanlike. Above its shaggy lowliness, as above a rusticated ground storey, rises the *piano nobile* of inset songs (April, August, November). Here, and in only a few other passages, the *Calendar* displays a liquid ease and subtlety of movement adequate to the brilliant rhetoric:

> Why do we longer live, (ah why live we so long) . . . ?
> (November 73; cf. 81, 111)

Note how the *correctio*, or restatement, puts a different accent on *we* and *live*, reinforcing the meaning yet also making a tenderly elegiac music. In such passages Spenser achieves a remarkably mellifluous flow. His special gift was for counter-pointing a great many structures and textures: rhetorical, phonetic, metrical. So in

> The mantled meadows mourn,
> Their sundry colours turn.
> (November 128–9)

the lines are matched by their similar clause length, their words of equivalent syllables symmetrically distributed, their rhetorical parallelism, and their literal meaning; so that the switch from alliteration (monochromatic consonants) to assonance (monochromatic vowels) mimes the drab change of colour. Spenser's later verse is full of such correspondences, in which form continuously accompanies sense in a cere-mony of meaning. His smooth style, indeed, has so domi-nated taste that we take it for granted and hardly notice the first beginnings. These should not be exaggerated either. The *Calendar* is high art, certainly; but only locally higher than that of Sidney. Overall, it is the *Calendar*'s ambitious encyclopedic content that bodes well, not its poetic language. It already shows a very special combination of complicated medieval structure with Renaissance hyperconsciousness about consistency. But it has attracted too much attention for the good of Spenser's modern reputation.

Spenser continued to write pastoral throughout his life. In 1591 *Astrophel: a Pastoral Elegy* appeared as the framing introduction to a volume of elegies on Sidney. Certainly later than 1586, and probably later than 1590, it is a finer work than most of *The Shepherd's Calendar*; although it has not usually been valued so highly. The first part (lines 1–216) relates, under the allegory of a boar-hunt, Sidney's death from a wound received at the battle of Zutphen (1586). Astrophel is gored by one of 'the brutish nation' (Spanish oppressors); mourned by his widow; and metamorphosed to a flower. This part, while always felicitous, preserves so impersonal a tone as to seem now a shade pallid, a little too consciously Bionesque. It is another matter with the Lay of Clorinda. This part, exactly half as long as the first—the proportions of harmony—purports to give the mourning song of Sidney's sister Mary, Countess of Pembroke. It is a deeply serious expression of grief, from which Milton learnt for *Lycidas*. Who is the mourner to address? She can hope for comfort neither from men nor from gods ('From them comes good, from them comes also ill'); so that she addresses her complaint to herself:

> The woods, the hills, the rivers shall resound
> The mournful accent of my sorrow's ground.
>
> (lines 23–4)

The resonance of *ground* ('ground-bass'; 'basis') is characteristic of the Lay's self-referring style, which can be poignant—as in 'The fairest flower . . . Was Astrophel; that *was*, we all may rue'. The resolution in this second part is deeper and darker: Clorinda reflects that when we grieve we may be self-regarding, 'Mourning in others, our own miseries'. Sidney is better where he is. If this part was by Mary herself (as some have suggested), she wrote a better poem than Spenser on this occasion.

In December 1591, from Kilcolman, Spenser dedicated to Sir Walter Raleigh *Colin Clout's Come Home Again*, a pastoral eclogue about a recent visit to court. This popular yet incompletely appreciated work is directly autobiographical, if not so literally as some have thought (it transports Gabriel Harvey, surely in wish-fulfilment, to Ireland). Its engaging method is that of general conversation, with no fewer than ten shepherds and shepherdesses interrupting and questioning Colin. These familiar exchanges establish a sense of Spenser's social and literary circle. They also, by their distancing or alienating effect, allow transitions through a wide range of tones, from the strangely exalted to the quietly humorous. The humour of Colin's account of his voyage is quite broad: sea ('A world of waters heaped up on high'), ships ('Glued together with some subtle matter') and myth-ologized admirals (Triton and Proteus) are consistently described as they might appear to an innocent, quite unironic shepherd's eye. Less obvious is the joke whereby the most extensive piece of alliteration—lines 25-6—comes in a speech of Hobbinol's. Harvey disliked the figure.

Most good eclogues are deeper than they look; and this one, probably the longest and most complex in the language, is no exception. It has an elaborate symmetrical structure to reflect its various but carefully balanced moods. There is even an inset eclogue, an account of a previous conversation with Raleigh 'the Shepherd of the Ocean', in which the narrative's doubly reported status expresses the remoteness of a primitive river-myth of sexual rivalry in the far past. The first half is divided between nature (the watery wilder-ness; wild Ireland) and art (epitomized by a catalogue of England's twelve chief poets). This passage, where Spenser authoritatively reviews his literary milieu and freely reveals his tastes, has an interest similar to that of, say, Auden's *Letter from Iceland*. Most praise goes to Daniel and Alabaster (both named), to Astrophel, to Alcyon (Sir Arthur Gorges) and to the mysterious Aetion. The second half answers with a catalogue of twelve ladies, courteously praised, and a lofty encomium of the Queen. Why then did Colin ever leave the court? His reply offsets the gallantry with a sharp attack on the court's incivility: 'it is no sort of life', and all its glory is 'but smoke, that fumeth soon away'. Hobbinol speaks up for Leicester, giving a well-informed review of his patronage programme; but Colin responds with renewed attacks, this time on the court's immorality.

All this has been seen as Spenser's ambivalence; and so in a way it may have been, in personal terms. But the poem's effect seems not so much ambiguous as poised. Peaceful England is excellent, by comparison with disordered Ireland:

the court is frivolous, by comparison with true civility. More delicately poised still is Colin's balance of Rosalind's cruelty to him with the queen's to Raleigh (whose suffering carries conviction—'Ah my love's queen, and goddess of my life'). He even reconciles a near-blasphemous panegyric of Elizabeth with elevation of another vassalage to a higher place within the poem's little world. Its sovereign centre honours not the queen, but the courteous grace of an un-named 'maid' (probably Elizabeth Throckmorton, later Lady Raleigh), to whom Spenser pays ardent homage:

> And I hers ever only, ever one:
> One ever I all vowed hers to be,
> One ever I, and other's never none.

(lines 477–9, of 955)

'Ever one . . . one ever . . . one ever' is no mere decorative rhetoric of chiasmus[1] or anaphora[2], but mimes the icono-graphic attitude of the three Graces, one facing forwards, two turned in outgoing. For the rest, the poem glances at several of the main interests of Spenser's mature work: cosmogonic myth; a metaphysic of 'Beauty the burning lamp of heaven's light'; and a passionate theology of love, with a myth of the Androgynous Venus. He condemns the court's lewdness not from a puritanical standpoint, but because it profanes the 'mighty mysteries' of love, 'that dread lord'. The poem's range of feeling is immense: no work gives a better sense of the possibilities of eclogue.

IV

In *Amoretti and Epithalamion* (1595) Spenser lays aside the pastoral weeds of Colin Clout to sing in his own person, as the lover of Elizabeth Boyle. Considering his early reputa-tion as a love poet, it is strange how few now think him one

---

[1] A figure of speech in which the word order in one phrase is inverted in another phrase soon after.

[2] The repetition of a word or phrase at the beginning of successive clauses or verses.

of the great sonneteers. The *Amoretti* can easily seem low pressure work, lacking the dramatic intensity of Sidney's *Astrophel and Stella*. However, interest grows when one appreciates how far Spenser's quieter virtues and more deeply poetic qualities have been missed. Take *Amoretti* 18, for example, in which the lover complains that whereas 'The rolling wheel ... The hardest steel in tract of time doth tear' and raindrops wear the 'firmest flint', yet he cannot move his lady. Stock images of obduracy; but how originally and deceptively they are put to work. Is the lady really discouraging? If tears are 'but water', then the proverb holds, and she will yield: only if tears contrasted with rain, would she be unmoved. Similarly when she '*turns* herself to laughter', who now is 'the rolling wheel' and who 'doth still remain'? Again, what association have flint and steel together, but kindled fire? The poetic indirection here is quite unlike anything in the other sonneteers of Spenser's time.

And in deeper ways too he is unlike them. Indeed, he came late enough in the vogue—after a dozen other English sonnet sequences'—to have to offer something different. Shakespeare responded to a similar challenge by writing sonnets that seem to be about friendship and jealousy. But Spenser's are not about passion at all, in the ordinary sense, but about a love that ends happily, in marriage: the British romantic love, mingling friendship with sexual desire, in praise of which he wrote at greater length in *The Faerie Queen*. The lover of the *Amoretti* (partly followed by the reader) gets to know Elizabeth Boyle well, forming a full personal relation with her. And a keenly intelligent, witty person she is—an Elizabeth Bennett rather than a Penelope Rich—with a firm, unmistakeable character. Unlike the usual Petrarchist lady, who is a trigger of passion and little else, Elizabeth does not wound with Cupid's darts, but calms passion's storm (8), and, characterized herself by 'goodly temperature' (13), frames and tempers her lover's feelings too. Even after they are mutually committed, in 84, we hear of her 'too constant stiffness'. This intense but tender courtship of a young girl by a middle aged lover has the air of reality. (The general situation is probably autobiographical: in *Amoretti* 60 Spenser implies that he is forty; and Elizabeth in fact outlived him, to have children by a second marriage at dates that make it likely that she was at least fifteen years younger.) Their love is deep, but too serious, too responsible, for passion.

Nevertheless, Elizabeth must receive every tribute usually paid to a slavishly worshipped sonneteer's goddess. In performing this contract Spenser shows an astonishing capacity to fulfil the forms of love complaint, and yet all the time to be free from them, above them—not so much through irony or travesty (although these are sometimes not far away) as through the direct, open refusal of conventional literary attitudes. To the latter, he prefers the more complex human comedy. Sometimes, it is true, he carries the Petrarchist commonplaces far enough towards absurdity to expose their false logic; as in 32: 'What then remains but I to ashes burn . . . ?' But more often the commonplaces—the fire and ice, the tyrant and captive, the storm and cruel tigress—are taken up with just a hint of distancing humour, a bantering tone or self-deprecating smile, to remind us that they belong to only one of the ways of wooing. The lover knows Elizabeth too well to think that she is really a tigress (in that way, at least). Not that the pains of love are merely acted, in a sense that would make them unreal. Indeed, where the idea of acting becomes most explicit, in the theatrical conceit of 54, the lady—who as unmoved spectator does not act—sits admonished: she is less than alive: 'a senseless stone'. Alternatively, the commonplaces may be taken up seriously but transformed. So it is with the erotic 'blazon', or item-by-item portrait, which had generated much loose poetry, particularly in French and Italian. Spenser has extremely sensuous sonnets of this type, such as the complete blazon in 64. There are several on Elizabeth's eyes, hair and breasts. In each case, however, the idea is elevated. In 76, her breasts are a 'bower of bliss', *pome acerbe* (unripe apples), 'like early fruit in May', between which the lover's frail thoughts dive 'through amorous insight'. But the very next sonnet shows the same apples in a dream, now ripe and 'golden', laid out for a sacred feast. For they surpass even those that Hercules came by in the Hesperidean garden of chastity: 'Sweet fruit of pleasure brought from paradise/By love himself'. It is the exalted desire of the *Song of Solomon*. Meanwhile, as he waits and woos, the lover is concerned to allay Elizabeth's anxiety about the loss of freedom that marriage would involve:

> The doubt which ye misdeem, fair love, is vain,
> That fondly fear to lose your liberty,
> When losing one, two liberties ye gain,
> And make him bond that bondage erst did fly.
> Sweet be the bands, the which true love doth tie,
> Without constraint or dread of any ill:
> The gentle bird feels no captivity
> Within her cage, but sings and feeds her fill.
> There pride dare not approach, nor discord spill [destroy]
> The league 'twixt them, that loyal love hath bound:
> But simple truth and mutual good will,
> Seeks with sweet peace to salve each other's wound:
> There faith doth fearless dwell in brazen tower,
> And spotless pleasure builds her sacred bower.
>
> (*Amoretti* 65)

There is a tenderness and reciprocity of feeling here that would be impossible to match anywhere else in the Renaissance sonnet.

Spenser could hardly have given such a love simple dramatic expression. Instead of Sidney's individually intense sonnets forming moments in a narrative, he has written what seems much more obviously a long stanzaic poem (as is expressed formally by linked rhyme-schemes). This continuity between sonnets, allowing complex large-scale imagery and amplitude of thematic development, goes back beyond the Petrarchists to the prolonged meditations of Petrarch's *Rime* themselves. Like Petrarch (and like Shakespeare) Spenser uses a calendrical structure to suggest the variety and natural growth of emotion. Thus there are New Year and Easter sonnets, set in their appropriate numerological places. The contradictory feelings that some have seen as problematic or indicative of revision all belong to this 'whole year's work', leading to the marriage day celebrated in *Epithalamion*. Like other Elizabethan 'sonnet sequences', *Amoretti* is really part of a composite work, combining sonnets with other stanza forms. Linking it to *Epithalamion* are four 'anacreontic odes' or sweet epigrams, which languish for the bliss of the wedding night. These serve as a generic transition to the major ode that follows.

Amoretti may fascinate as an interesting departure from the usual sequence, or as a shorter treatment of themes developed in *The Faerie Queen*. But *Epithalamion* is unique. Nothing shows Spenser's creativity better than this poem, which most agree to be the finest major ode in English, and to be surpassed in ancient literature, if at all, only by Pindar. Classical comparisons are inevitable, because Spenser here invented for English literature the humanist ceremonial mode that was to be so important for Drayton, Herrick and others—and carried it at once to its greatest height. Like Catullus' *Carmina* 61, Spenser's poem moves in festal exaltation through the events of a wedding day. But its structure is very different; rising as it does through a crescendo of gathering voices and sounds and excitement to the roaring organs and public affirmation of the marriage service at the altar, in the central two stanzas or strophes; before the feasting, the public 'bedding' of the bride, consummation and soft recession into the silence and darkness of the night. Each stage is due and accepted:

> Now welcome night, thou night so long expected,
> That long day's labour dost at last defray,
> And all my cares, which cruel love collected,
> Hast summed in one, and cancelled for aye:
> Spread thy broad wing over my love and me,
> That no man may us see,
> And in thy sable mantle us unwrap,
> From fear of peril and foul horror free.
> Let no false treason seek us to entrap,
> Nor any dread disquiet once annoy
> The safety of our joy:
> But let the night be calm and quietsome,
> Without tempestuous storms or sad affray:
> Like as when Jove with fair Alcmena lay,
> When he begot the great Tirynthian groom:
> Or like as when he with thy self did lie,
> And begot Majesty.
> And let the maids and youngmen cease to sing:
> Ne let the woods them answer nor their echo ring.
>
> (Stanza 18)

What audacity, for a poet to dare to speak to the goddess Night about her lovemaking!—and yet how apt, at the juncture when he is about to become intimate with his own wife. Throughout, mythological imagery mingles with real, external with psychological. Indeed, the comprehensiveness takes in even negative feelings, such as dread of an 'affray', and sexual fears of 'Medusa's mazeful head'. Spenser's robust yet sensitive personal address is unflinchingly inclusive, as he faces both day and unconscious night in the ritual of love. His ceremony remains reverent; yet it affirms nature and finds authenticity in the role of Jupiter, spouse of Night. These and other deep archetypes and powers are recognized and profoundly composed: the *Horae*, the *Gratiae*, the *amorini* of passion, Cynthia the chaste destroyer yet patroness of childbirth, and, in the one stanza, Juno foundress of marriage and female genius, together with Genius himself, god of pleasure and generation. As Spenser invokes them in turn, or turns from one wedding scene to another, he dwells on each in such a way that the stanzas acquire their own characters and modalities. They are like the dances of a suite. Now all is private communing with the 'learned sisters'; now expectant bachelors wait for Hymen's torchlit masque to move off; now pristine garlanded 'nymphs' make final arrangements. One stanza will be a blazon of Elizabeth's beauties admired by all ('lips like cherries charming men to bite'): the next a mysterious praise of her chaste inner character. The poem's movement through this variety is fluid but calm and firm and sure. It is as if everything had its inevitable place.

And so, in numerological terms, it had. The spatial disposition of *Epithalamion* mimes with extraordinary precision the astronomical events of the day it celebrates. Thus the 24 stanzas represent its 24 hours, with night falling at the right point for St Barnabas' Day, the summer solstice, 'the longest day in all the year'. Then, after Stanza 16, the refrain changes from positive to negative: 'The woods no more shall answer, nor your echo ring'. And the *canzone*-like stanzas consist of pentameters and occasional trimeters, with the long lines numbering just 365 to represent the days of the year, during which the sun completes his journey round the 24 sidereal hours. The ceremony of time has never been realized so fully as in this most musical of Spenser's poems. It is indeed an 'endless monument' to the poignantly short time of his day. Yet before the end it has carried the torches of its masque up to join the 'thousand torches flaming bright' in the temple of the gods. It aspires to commemorate an anticipated cosmic event, addition to the communion of saints, eventual 'stellification'.

Prothalamion (1596), written for an aristocratic betrothal, has similar ceremonial qualities and a form almost as highly wrought. It too is a masterpiece of occasional art in the grand mannerist style. But, in spite of autobiographical references to 'old woes', it is more public, more philosophical and harder at first to warm to. Only after prolonged consideration and the effort of attending to its closely overdetermined images does its profundity emerge. It not only sums up the whole river epithalamium genre, but sings the mutability of the height of life. Spenser wrote other short works, notably the medievalizing satire *Mother Hubberd's Tale* and the lofty Christian-Platonic *Hymns*. The former is not dull; but neither does it show Spenser to have been a great satirist. As for the *Hymns*, they challenge more attention, as a vastly ambitious undertaking, a poetic theology of love and generation. Their extreme difficulty (and the correspondingly glorious opportunity they offer to the commentator) is not their only interest for Spenserians. They cast much cloudy light on Spenser's unexpected, syncretistic thinking. But this is not enough to make them great poems. Whether their metaphysical puzzles yield to solution or remain attributed to blunders, the *Hymns* must be counted noble failures. When all is said and done (and much has still to be said, for the love poems particularly), the work in which Spenser chiefly lives is *The Faerie Queen*.

V

The Faerie Queen occupies a very special place in English literature. Yet far more would acknowledge its classic status than would count themselves among its readers. There are doubtless several reasons for this, some of which I mention below. One may be a misconception about the kind of work *The Faerie Queen* is. Another, closely related, may be the disablement inflicted by much reading of 'probable report' novels, which seems to produce insensitivity to less novelistic sorts of fictive realism. A third may be its length. For my own part, I was fortunate enough to come upon the poem during a convalescence: I could read without interruption. But there are other ways of reading such a work, which were not unknown to the Elizabethans themselves. In his translation of *Orlando Furioso* Sir John Harington gives directions 'for the several tales, where to begin and end, those that may conveniently be read single'. Of course such a method will not give a very adequate idea of the work, unless it is complemented by reading *in extenso*. Much of the characteristic quality of *The Faerie Queen* depends on juxtaposition of stories and episodes of different kinds: on interrupted, interwoven narrative, on multiplication.

And this is perhaps the first point to take hold of: that it is a work of interlaced art. Suppose you are following the story of Belphoebe. You pick it up in Book 2, Canto 3, Stanzas 21–42, a luscious ten-stanza description of the heroine, broken up by a comic encounter with Trompart and the upstart Braggadocchio. Belphoebe explains that true honour comes by hard work, and is more likely to be found in the forest (or studying at home) than at court. But when she has fiercely rebuffed an improper advance, and fled, she makes no further appearance in this Book—nor in the next, until 3.5.57, where she cares for the wounded Timias. Her parentage and relation to Amoret are explained in the canto following, through the myth of Chrysogone. But then she disappears again until Book 4, by which time several other stories have been woven into the fabric. If the reader loses track of these windings he should on no account despair: all is going according to plan: the sense of labyrinthine unsearchability is a desired effect. Some degree of incomprehension is as deliberate a feature in Spenser's art as it is in certain types of medieval romance, or in the visual interlace of the *Book of Kells*. The reader may follow the pattern again and again, and have the experience, as in life, of gradual understanding.

To enjoy Spenser's *entrelacement*, feel free, first, to reread. Second, attend closely to the distant connections (whether of resemblance, variation, or contrast) between widely separate parts of the poem. As in most interlaced narratives, such internal allusions carry a great deal of the content. Third, notice the transitions between stories and between episodes. It is often at these points of juncture that Spenser indicates the fictive status of the various milieux which are brought into relation, and implies a deeper import. So the beautiful description of achieved true honour, Belphoebe alone, confronts the farcical pretentions of Braggadocchio (a thin character), and his sycophant. And this scene is in turn followed by Guyon's adventures on quite a different scale— far more minutely psychological—as he overcomes a series of difficulties in the pursuit of honour. The formal relation of interlaced narrative strands can offer a pleasure of its own, like that of abstract art. But with Spenser the interruptions of the story generally also give reminders of farther reality. The breaks in his tapestry disclose glimpses of windows that look out on larger, more complex worlds. When Artegall returning victorious encounters the Blatant Beast (5.12.37) the juncture of stories shows how military and administrative success are not enough: there is also a social world, with reputation to be won or lost. In this sense, polyphonic narrative serves the deeper purpose of comprehensiveness, of inclusiveness, of Renaissance epic's aspiration to complete unity. It is not quite the same as *entrelacement* in the older romances.

At one time, *The Faerie Queen* used to be thought of as the last great medieval work in English, although it was also supposed to have been written without much access to medieval literature. Now the manner of its medievalism is more problematic. Many would agree that Spenser knew Malory, together with other late romances. And there can be no doubt at all of his respect for old traditions: of his deep passion for 'old records from ancient times derived' and of his avidity, as greedy as Guyon's, for romantic antiquities—chronicles and armour and heraldry and ruins and hermitages. *Ancient*—or, even older, *auncient*—is indeed one of his favourite words, which he is capable of using twice in the same line: 'Ancient Ogyges, even the ancientest'. There is some justice in C. S. Lewis's view that Spenser was 'the first of the romantic medievalists'. Certainly the retrospective Gothic taste in literature was identified from the start (in Pope and Warton for example) with a taste for *The Faerie Queen*. It should not be forgotten, however, that Spenser's own medieval enthusiasm was also coupled with a rather sharp stylishness. We miss a great deal of what he was about unless we appreciate his sophisticated modernity too. Not that Spenser was ever a merely fashionable writer. But he wrote in part 'to overgo Ariosto', who had established a vogue for Gothic costume narrative. It might be more accurate to characterize *The Faerie Queen* as mannerist neo-Gothic, rather than medieval. This stylistic character is reflected in the form, which is not romance, but romantic epic.

Epic was supposed to give a sense of life's totality. And each Renaissance epicist in turn aimed at farther, fuller inclusiveness, both by reaching out to a progressively more diverse or encyclopedic content, and by subsuming, whether through allusion or other means, contents already enclosed in the poetic domain of previous epics. Thus the commentators taught that Virgil's *Aeneid* combined an *Odyssey* (Books 1–6) with an *Iliad* (7–12). Moreover, Scaliger and other literary theorists had developed the doctrine that epic contains a wide variety of inset smaller forms. Spenser gave a creative turn to this idea: anticipating Milton's *Paradise Lost*, he included several different epic and romance forms in *The Faerie Queen*. Ariostan epic—all scramble and bravura and surprise—is probably his principal Italian ingredient. But he also uses Tasso's larger scale, especially for elaborate set pieces with luxuriant detail, such as the Bower of Bliss. Then there are passages of obscure Boiardan epic, burlesque and puns like Pulci's, and even a few static hieroglyphs reminiscent of Trissino's *L'Italia Liberata da Gotti*. Ancient epic is represented not only in its Virgilian form (complete with descents into hell, games, extended similes and stylistic formulae of the sort that Ford Madox Ford called 'marmoreal Latinisms'), but also in its Ovidian (metamorphoses and loves of the gods). And it would risk Polonius's folly to enumerate the other types, such as pastoral epic, meandering through the world of the *Aethiopica* and the *Arcadia*; allegorical quests distantly resembling Deguilleville's or Hawes's; and (in the Cantos of Mutability) a procession like the ones in Du Bartas's Christian epic of creation.

All this should not be taken to mean that Spenser merely pillaged Biblical, classical, medieval and Renaissance epics for source material. His sources are a separate topic, which hardly lends itself to brief treatment, being so poorly understood. Some of the poetical sources are beyond doubt. But the informational sources may have been fewer and more compendious, murkier and less literary, than scholars have assumed. Allusion would be a better term than borrowing: Spenser is the first great allusive poet in English. And his mastery of generic variation goes farther than I have suggested. With never a hint of pastiche, he deploys different kinds, almost as a composer scores for different instruments, to render life's various modes. Spenser is not always superior in handling a particular form. Ariosto's adventures, for example, run more easily; although Spenser's come very close in such an episode as Timias's skirmish with the foresters (3.5), and in any case are carrying more weight. But in shading such adventures into writing of other kinds, in using his far wider generic palette, in mixture, Spenser shows fictive genius of a different order altogether.

VI

The detachment of *The Faerie Queen* from previous epics is reflected in its decisive formal individuation. Its metre, the 'Spenserian Stanza', that great legacy to Thomson and Shelley and Keats, contrives to be at once novel and traditional. By comparison with the brisk heroic stanza of Ariosto and Tasso, *ottava rima*—*a b a b a b c c*—the larger English stanza is spacious and unhurried; while its more intricately interlaced rhymes—*a b a b b c b c c*—further slow its pace (usually: exceptions include the sprightly cadence at 7.7.46), and knit it more closely together. The final alexandrine, which determines much of the effect of stateliness and weight, allows us to think not only of a nine-line stanza, but of an eight-line stanza rounded off: *a b a b b c b c C*—the ballade or *Monk's Tale* stanza, in fact, extended and transcended. Chaucer's stanza consists of two separate, symmetrical, couplet-linked halves: *a b a b/b c b c*. But the notional halves of the indivisible Spenserian stanza are united by its shared central line:

> *a b a b b*
> *b c b c C.*

An Elizabethan critic describing it—as Drayton described his own *Barons' Wars* stanza—might also have observed how it rests like a column on its hexameter base (six feet, a number of perfection), or how its rhymes occur 2, 3, and 4 times: the numbers grouped by Macrobius and others as forming the ratios of the fundamental musical concords.

> Right in the midst the goddess' self did stand
> Upon an altar of some costly mass,
> Whose substance was uneath [difficult] to understand:
> For neither precious stone, nor dureful brass,
> Nor shining gold, nor mouldering clay it was;
> But much more rare and precious to esteem,
> Pure in aspéct, and like to crystal glass,
> Yet glass was not, if one did rightly deem,
> But being fair and brickle [brittle], likest glass did seem.
>
> (4.10.39)

The Spenserian stanza has been well compared to a wave falling on a beach: breaking, it runs to implement the full alexandrine mark and to give, where needed, a meditative lull. It 'closeth not but with a full satisfaction to the ear for so long detention'. It is the greatest of all stanzas.

The Italianate division into cantos tends to be taken for granted; but it was an innovation in English. Spenser offset it against a different division, of antique association, into books. Within each book, the cantos may vary greatly in representational mode. This is indeed the poem's most copious source of variety. It relies on formal variegation more than on multiplication of narrative incident.

This point calls for enlargement. The stanza just quoted, describing a mysterious altar of Venus, comes from a canto about Scudamour's entry into the Temple of Venus, a fully realized allegorical place in the manner of medieval dream vision. Book Four in general treats friendship; but this canto initiates us into the very sanctum of the virtue, its inner nature, foundation, ideals, meaning. In the same way, each book has some such medullar or 'core' canto, in which, usually, the champion of a virtue visits a place that symbolizes its essential character. St. George the patron of Holiness visits the House of Holiness in 1.10; Guyon, the patron of Temperance, the castle of Alma in 2.9; and Artegall, Mercilla's Court in 5.9. In such cantos the virtue is developed visually through an orderly procession, a pageant tableau, or its descriptive equivalent. It is a special symbolic mode that goes back to medieval vision allegories. Valuations of it now differ sharply, usually according to the critic's familiarity with its subtle conventions. But few would question that in the fiction of a Chaucer or a Colonna or a Spenser it can be a profoundly eloquent, although very oblique form. The expressionist mysteriousness of the Garden of Adonis or the Temple of Venus is quite unlike almost anything in Ariosto: it is more like the enigmatic *Hypnerotomachia*, that strange work of sexual mysticism, whose psychological intuitions fascinated many writers and artists of the Renaissance. We can try to explain some features of Spenser's symbolic places. It may help to compare the material of Venus' altar with the rich shining substance of the Fountain of Will in the Bower of Bliss (2.12.60), or to know that in erotic poetry glass might figure the female pudendum (e.g. *Greek Anthology* 5.36). But schematic interpretation of the Temple of Venus would be unthinkable. Too much is deeply implicit, or indirectly conveyed, for that. How is the brittle glass related to Ptolomaee's glass tower of marital fidelity at 3.2.20? And Phidias, whose Paphian idol is introduced to amplify the greater beauty of this living god: does his wretched love for a mere image belong with the many unhappy loves about the altar? Again, why do the lovers outside the Temple sport their pleasures, while those within, and closest to the strange hermaphroditic goddess, suffer and complain? If Spenser invites such questions, he does not encourage quick answers.

The strange symbolic places stand out prominently, each like a *temenos* or sanctuary or *arcanum* set in the deep forest of romance. But they form one kind of episode only, one component of the Spenserian book. Another sort, coming in an early position, serves to join the adventures and to show the relations between the virtues that the knights strive for. Thus Redcrosse, patron of holiness, and Guyon, patron of temperance, meet and almost fight at 2.1.26; and Britomart (chaste love) shows herself superior to Guyon in a trial of strength at 3.1.6. Then there are early passages that announce the book's subjects by developing emblems of the virtues in their abstract or common acceptation: St. George's encounter with Error in 1.2, Guyon's visit to Medina's castle of moderation in 2.1, Cambina's reconciliation of combatants in 4.3. These passages pose the books' topics in broad terms. The subjects thus stated undergo modification as well as expansion, however; so that the virtues of the early emblems are by no means identical with those realized in the 'core cantos'. The latter present insights only reached after the experience (i.e. adventures) of attempting the virtue. As for the intervening adventures themselves, they superficially appear like Ariosto's. But in reality they also contribute a medieval (or medievalizing) element. They have a far more continuous moral sense than the adventures of most romances—even of many medieval romances. The Spenserian hero encounters obstacles to his virtue, or aspects of the opposing vice, which are thus analysed into branches or subdivisions like those familiar from older moral works such as Frère Lorens's *Somme le Roi*. (Sometimes the categories are surprising and thought-provoking; as when Sansloy, a brother of Sansfoy and Sansjoy, developed characters in Book 1, makes a perfunctory appearance in Book 2 on the quite different scale of an aberration from Medina's golden mean.) Certain of the vices are explored fully enough to call for 'places' of their own, such as the Cave of Mammon

(2.7) or the House of Busirane (3.11–12). Finally, there are 'digressive' episodes, such as the inset chronicle histories at the Castle of Alma and the river-god spousals of Thames and Medway, or the subplot adventures of Florimell, Marinell and Belphoebe.

If some such repertoire of forms gives variety within a book, each book has nevertheless its own individual character. And each seems so distinct in emotional key as to compose with the others a sequence of complementary movements. The apocalyptic Book 1 runs a vast gamut of spiritual extremities, from dark to light. But in Book 2 we move to a world at once more schematically controlled and more sensuously vivid, with a tendency to frequent confrontations between its single (almost single-minded) hero and his many, minutely problematic emotions. Book 3's ardours are in the ordinary proportion of romance. Its characters disperse in ramifying adventures; but they are re-gathered by the centripetal tendency of Book 4, through which accumulating groups of four friends (true or false) join by aggregation in a movement towards the great nuptial feast of Thames and Medway. Book 5 is Draconian in its severity. But Book 6 is unbraced and vulnerable, its knights disarmed or dressed in shepherds' clothes. Throughout, the atmosphere alters in the interests of variety, and alters again for a balanced view of the wholeness of human experience.

Perhaps for the same reason, the emotional colorations change without any hard-edged divisions. They shade into one another with a subtlety and delicacy that is one of the chief marks of Spenser's art. He seems to achieve the effect partly by running stories and themes over to blur the divisions, by arranging trailers or anticipations of any change of mood, and by suturing in the overlaps with an astonishing fineness and obliquity. (Metrically this finds reflection in a system of liaison of rhyme between stanzas.) Thus, although *The Faerie Queen* is manneristically composite and complicated outwardly, as a reading experience it is not like that at all. Inwardly it moves with an almost baroque fluidity. Its wonderful transitions, for example, have none of the alienating abruptness of Ariosto's, which, as scholars have noted, go back to medieval formulae such as 'Mes a tant laisse

33

li contes a parler de . . . et retorne a . . .' ('Now I leave off the story of . . . and return to . . .'). Instead we move by a smooth, imperceptible progression from episode to episode, mode to mode, with even the explicit junctures, where these occur, accomplishing more than a mere narrative cut and join.

Thus, 3.6 begins with the geniture of Belphoebe and her twinship with Amoret—an inset Ovidian tale of Chrysogone provides the canto's first mythological treatment of generation, inside an *occupatio* (a pretended refusal to discuss):

> It were a goodly story, to declare,
> By what strange accident fair Chrysogone
> Conceived these infants, and how them she bare,
>
> (3.6.5)

—and then slides into a lost Cupid myth. This naturally leads to a burlesque quarrel between the distraught Venus and the at first censorious, then relenting Diana, until their accord brings discovery of the twin births of Belphoebe and Amoret, and arrangements for their separate fostering: a separation that implies an emotional polarity corresponding to that which exists between the traditionally opposed goddesses (11–28). Cupid has been found, divided or 'unfolded' into two forms. Then an apparently casual transition takes us into the famous Garden of Adonis: 'She brought her to her joyous Paradise,/Where most she wones [stays], when she on earth does dwell.' (3.6.29). Besides introducing a second mythological treatment of generation, however, this stanza adds a psychological, individually sexual strand, by its personal confession:

> Whether in Paphos, or Cytheron hill,
> Or it in Gnidus be, I wot not well;
> But well I wot by trial, that this same
> All other pleasant places doth excel, . . .

In the Garden itself (30–50), the metaphysical, physical and mythic elements interweave with formidable ease yet without ever seeming clever—suggesting, rather, Virgil's profundity of feeling and suggestion.

34

There wont fair Venus often to enjoy
Her dear Adonis' joyous company,
And reap sweet pleasure of the wanton boy;
There yet, some say, in secret he does lie,
Lappèd in flowers and precious spicery,
By her hid from the world, and from the skill
Of Stygian gods, which do her love envy;
But she her self, when ever that she will,
Possesseth him, and of his sweetness takes her fill.

And sooth it seems they say: for he may not
For ever die, and ever buried be
In baleful night, where all things are forgot;
All be he subject to mortality,
Yet is etern in mutability,
And by succession made perpetual,
Transformèd oft, and changèd diversely:
For him the father of all forms they call;
Therefore needs mote [must] he live, that living gives to all.

(3.6.46–7)

The Garden is where an individual participates, through the
act of sex, in making new life; and where the relation of
form and matter, of permanence and change, declares itself. It is a Christian-Platonic-Pythagorean vision of the
soul's vocation in a world of accident. At the same time, the
canto is full of Spenser's own characteristic bitter-sweet
cheerful melancholy. Wicked Time destroys the Garden's
goodly things; but the pity of that cannot make it other
than a gloriously creative place. Time's scythe mows; but
Venus can still 'reap sweet pleasure'. The canto began with
explanation of Belphoebe's inherited qualities, which led,
through the confrontation of Venus and Diana, to the Garden
of Adonis. But Spenser leaves the Garden for the story of
Belphoebe's vulnerable twin, Amoret (52–3), and then,
by a more distant modulation, for that of the still more
fearful Florimell. We have moved from Belphoebe almost
to her opposite, with hardly a break.

VII

The movement of *The Faerie Queen* seems fluid and un-predictable, almost like human experience. To get this realistic effect it must avoid obvious regularities of the composite parts. Consequently order, although everywhere discoverable, is everywhere hidden. Thus, placement of the so-called core cantos varies from book to book: 1.10, 4.10 and 6.10, but 2.9 and 5.9. Yet the variation is not random either, since it follows a number symbolism: the core cantos in ninth place enshrine cardinal virtues, Temperance and Justice. Similarly, the contents of books broadly follow the sequence of the planetary week, with Book 1 as the Book of Sol, Book 2 as Luna, and so forth. Truth (troth, faith), the subject of Book 1, was a usual association or meaning of the sun; just as Una's lion attendant—the ter-rible aspect of truth—would have been recognized as Sol's astrological house. The planetary series is interrupted, however, when Book 3 proves to be not a Book of Mars, but of his feminine and wiser counterpart Minerva (a cult image of Queen Elizabeth). The overall narrative pattern of yearly quests shows a similarly regular irregularity. St. George's mission against the dragon and Guyon's against Acrasia lead us to expect one adventure per book. But Books 3 and 4 have between them only one, Scudamour's. Again, most of the books feature the titular patron of a virtue, sent out from Gloriana's court. In Book 3, however, it is Britomart, not Scudamour, who defeats Busirane and frees Amoret; while Book 4 has two other heroes, Cambel and Triamond, who do not belong to Gloriana's order of knighthood. These variations can easily seem random and confused. But they turn out to be governed by a structural logic, related to Christian-Platonic or neo-Platonic concepts such as the Triad. The latter not only informs many group-ings of characters—Sansfoy, Sansjoy, Sansloy, etc.—but also a division, confirmed by the order of publication, into three-book parts.

Another structural pattern that runs throughout is the arrangement of thematic images in ascending sequence, from evil through less evil, or mixed, to good. In Book 6 the series is of human 'garlands' ranging from the cannibals gathered round Serena, through the lusty shepherds and lovely lasses round Pastorella, to the 'hundred naked maidens lily white, / All ranged in a ring' round the three Graces—who themselves encircle 'another damsel', Spenser's own love. The theme makes connection through the common figure of a garland, whose oblatory meaning becomes explicit in the primitive ritual (6.8.39, 6.9.8, 6.10.12 and 6.10.14). In the same way bad Venuses taking pleasure at the Bower of Bliss and the House of Malecasta precede the good Venus enjoying the Garden of Adonis. And the pains of a cruel Cupid triumphing at the House of Busirane (3.11–12) go before the painful sentence pronounced by the 'wise' Cupid at 6.8.22–5. It is a law of Fairyland. The quests are always making gradual labyrinthine approaches, or ascents in Platonic fashion, from perverse and dark images towards the reality of virtues themselves. The virtues have to be composed, step by step, in a process of integration. It is a remarkably inclusive vision. At the Temple of Venus are held in concord not only love and hate 'brethren both of half the blood' (4.10.32), but Venus and Cupid, potentially, and the pleasure and pain of love.

It is Spenser's Christian Platonism, his conception of things as images of reality, that makes sense of dwelling on symbolic objects rather than on probable action. Certainly *The Faerie Queen* is pictorial in the extreme. When Joseph Spence read it to his aged mother, she said that he 'had been showing her a collection of pictures'; and Pope appreciatively concurred. Not all post-Victorian critics have cared for this picturesque quality. Some have felt quite superior to the naïvety of speaking pictures. But we should remember that in the Renaissance—even partly in Ruskin's time—pictures spoke conceptually and articulately. Whether or not our ancestors were also in closer touch with the images of the unconscious, they demonstrably used a conscious and conventional iconographical language. The adventure of the champion of temperance is full of emblems of the virtue, such as the bridle or collar, which appears in the 'gorgeous barbs' of Guyon's horse Brigador (*briglia d'oro*), in the bridle put on Occasion's tongue, and perhaps in the elaborately described 'silken camus lily white' worn by Belphoebe (Latin *camus* 'bridle, collar'; English *camis* 'tunic'). Belphoebe also wore

> a golden baldric, which forelay
> Athwart her snowy breast, and did divide
> Her dainty paps; which like young fruit in May
> Now little gan to swell, and being tied,
> Through her thin weed their places only signified.
>
> (2.3.29)

The half-exposed bosom regularly emblemized true honour; so that an Elizabethan reader was prepared in advance to recognize the values latent in Belphoebe's confrontation with Braggadocchio and Trompart.

Spenser does not always give explanatory labels to such relatively simple iconography. And even when he seems explicit, as with the cruel hag Occasion, the labelling abstraction by no means exhausts the image's meaning. Literature dominated iconography, rather than the reverse: Spenser was forming images not yet in any handbook. His figure was not Occasion in general (who would have been a young girl) but a very specific Occasion, incorporating such additional features as the lameness of Poena (slow retribution). Possibly Spenser himself could not have identified the composite figure much more fully, in other terms than he has actually used. He was exploring psychological depths: the springs of impatience, the penalties of guilt. His emblematic pictures and hieroglyphs were not, after all, merely quaint, but a means to self-discovery. Having only a smattering of the language of emblem, our best approach is to meditate the scene as a whole, and to take in details of mood and appearance. We need to feel Occasion's intemperate readiness to blame—perhaps to guess at the suggestion of self-punishing remorse in the cruelty of her son Furor—before we know how to bring iconography to bear.

In a fiction that uses images as its words in this way, language is apt to be of secondary importance, at least compared with an epic such as *Paradise Lost*. I do not mean that *The Faerie Queen* is carelessly or flatly written. Its style can reach intensity when a grand theme calls for it; as in the description of

> Death with most grim and grisly visage seen,
> Yet is he nought but parting of the breath;
> Ne ought to see, but like a shade to ween [suppose],
> Unbodièd, unsouled, unheard, unseen.

(7.7.46)

And it varies with every change of mode: lyrical, narrative, descriptive. But much of the time it makes little conscious impression on the casual reader. Like the clean window glass that you do not notice so long as you focus on a distant object, the language of *The Faerie Queen* is usually transparent. Every now and then comes a more noticeable stanza, such as the intricately eloquent, densely patterned, much quoted description of the Cave of Sleep (1.1.41). But such 'opaqueness' is unrepresentative of a narrative style that mostly effaces itself. This shaven manner of the narrative allegory contrasts with the richer sonority of description sustained in the 'core' cantos. There, epiphanies stand out with the dense force of language of a major ode. The disparity is of course deliberate. For the discriminating reader, indeed, this balance of plane surfaces and enriched areas offers one of the main pleasures of the poem.

Not that the diction is neutral or colourless, even in the narrative allegory. It has too marked a medieval tinge for that. Still, the notorious archaisms are fewer and less frequent than critics suggest: many stanzas have none, and others have only the token *ne* or *eke* of the poem's soon-familiar idiolect. On the other hand, there is a good deal more sly word-play than used to be recognized. Sometimes Spenser draws on proverbial lore, which may provide the basis of a whole episode, in the manner of Langland or Nashe or Brueghel. But more often the wit takes the form of what Hazlitt called 'an allegorical play upon words': a punning ambiguity, that is, with one meaning in the story and the other in the allegory; as at 6.9.5, where Calidore, who brought the faults of the court with him in his courtly nature, enquires after the Blatant Beast, 'If such a beast they saw, which he had thither brought'. Altogether the language, which owes much in this to Gavin Douglas, brilliantly compounds the high flown and the vernacular.

VIII

I have left until now the problems of the allegory; since these have been exaggerated into unnecessary stumbling blocks. Victorian and Georgian critics were predisposed against what they saw as didactic and mechanical 'naïve allegory'. But Spenser's poem would now be generally exonerated from these charges. If its moral seems in any sense too bare, it is not in the sense of being crude or obvious. Besides, there is now more feeling for what was a dominant form of literature in the Middle Ages, and at least one of the most prominent in the Renaissance. Spenser, however, wrote a special sort of allegory, whose characteristics should be distinguished. He himself called *The Faerie Queen* 'a continued allegory, or dark conceit' and noticed 'how doubtfully all allegories may be construed' (Letter to Raleigh).

Like much Elizabethan criticism, this calls for sympathetic interpretation. When he calls the allegory 'continued', Spenser probably means that it is not merely local, but kept up by the author all through. In this his poem differs from, say, *Orlando Furioso*. Ariosto has occasional allegories, such as that of Logistilla; and he was freely *allegorized*, by such anti-intentionalists *des ses jours* as Fornari and Bononome. But Spenser wrote throughout what was meant allegorically or symbolically. Unlike the strange places and marvels of medieval romance (and, to a large extent, those in Ariosto), Spenser's are interpreted. In consequence they are brought into unity with the rest of the work. Thus, the Sixth Book's improbably numerous foundlings are not left as a matter of surprise and delightful wonder. Spenser makes it plain that the marvel, anything but arbitrary, is designed to explore various relations between natural inheritance and 'nurture' (environmental influences). To the various structures of the *Orlando*, therefore, *The Faerie Queen* adds another quite distinct.

Moreover, this extra strand is itself manifold. Unlike Bunyan's allegory (which has only one sphere of reference, the religious), Spenser's may be religious or moral or psychological or philosophical or political. Most often, perhaps, it is moral, setting out virtues and vices, or distinctions within virtues and vices, in the narrative mode by which ethics used to be understood. Lucifera and the Giant Orgoglio present different kinds of pride; the six knights of Malecasta six steps into lechery. Other figures, however, such as Pyrochles and Cymochles, or Elissa and Perissa, treat polarities of a more psychological order. In Shamefastness and Praise-desire, indeed, Spenser explores the springs of moral behaviour in two contrasting temperamental dispositions. It is often observed, and rightly, that his psychological insights seldom issue in character studies. But we should recall that each book really studies a single 'super-character', its hero, whose traits are the individual allegorical characters. (And the 'Letter to Raleigh' hints that Arthur himself composes a super-hero from the hero-parts of individual books.) Regarded in this light, Spenser's poem is seen to analyse psychological experience in unusual depth. Even so, some of his greatest passages tend in another direction altogether, belonging to a philosophical allegory enacted either by abstract personifications (Mutability) or by mythological figures (Adonis).

There is also, particularly in Book 5, a political allegory, which many have found repellent in its severity. The iron man Talus with his flail seems uncomfortably proleptic of the harshest modern riot police. What is one to think, in particular, of Spenser's attitude to Ireland? As a patriot, he worked for the English oppressors. Yet he hated violence and loved peace and justice. Such an attitude wins few friends now. It has even been asserted, by Yeats and others, that Spenser hated the Irish. The fact remains that in his prose *View of the Present State of Ireland* Spenser attempted what few British and American writers have emulated: to understand the Irish. It does not do to forget the magnitude of the disorders or the weakness of government in Spenser's time.

The allegory, of course, often has multiple implications. Indeed, the same character may have a political or topical, as well as a moral, meaning. Artegall, for example, combines Sovereign Power, Justice, and Maleness-in-generation (not portrayed as a superior role) with Leicester, Essex, Grey, and perhaps other historical figures. Similarly, Belphoebe represents Queen Elizabeth, but also Virginality. But in approaching these 'antique praises unto present persons fit' we must not be tempted into looking for a key. Such figures represent insights into life: they should not be reduced to system, but responded to with a correspondingly personal intuition.

This is true of all Spenser's allegories. You cannot be too subtle in interpreting them; but you can easily be subtle in the wrong way. Alertness is everything. In the Cave of Mammon episode, Guyon's refraining from combat with golden Disdain (who resembles 'an huge Giant') has attracted ingenious explanations. Guyon is learning that martial heroism is not enough, etc. But the alert reader will sense that the supercilious hero has blundered. Perhaps what prompts him is a remembered law of Fairyland, that Giants are for fighting (as witness Orgoglio, Argante, Ollyphant, Corflambo, the Giant with the Scales, Geryoneo and others). Or perhaps he reflects that Mammon's advice to 'abstain from perilous fight' is unlikely to be dependable. (Another law: evil figures give bad advice.) In any event, by not fighting Guyon has gone disastrously wrong. His moral heroism has degenerated into mere aristocratic *sdegno*: he is literally reconciled to disdain: and he rejects the world because he feels superior to it. He may be doing the right thing; but for the wrong reason. A really wakeful reader will also see Spenser's joke, that all the time golden Disdain is really 'non-U': a 'villain'. Such a point is a matter for the attention of the third ear. The laws of Fairyland are not those of deductive logic.

IX

No sooner has one drawn attention to the complicated manifold character of *The Faerie Queen* than the balance must be righted by affirming its simplicity. Mere formal complication seems almost irrelevant to Spenser's serious purpose: his sophisticated detachment from forms serves other than formal values. He uses any means that will illustrate the deepest truth of the matter. Hence his easy freedom with sources. Since he is more concerned with truth than with elegance or poetic success, great predecessors never intimidate him. He has had his own glimpse of life; and in the end it is for his unified vision that we read *The Faerie Queen*.

Spenser's reliance on chivalric values may appear to contradict what I have just written, and to make any very high seriousness impossible. How can we take seriously a knighthood that was already outgrown in the poet's own time—that he himself presents, indeed, in anachronistic terms? Well, a reinterpreted knighthood, offering ideals for courtiers and administrators, may have formed a part of Spenser's purpose. But it would be a mistake to think of this as merely an aspiration to some Indian summer of English chivalry. At the very least, the adventures are moral psychomachies. And their content is quite as much private as public. They continually press behind virtues to the growth of 'the fresh bud of virtue'; to the 'sacred nursery / Of virtue' 'deep within the mind'; and even to 'the root' of all virtue, in love (4 Proem 2). In Spenser, virtues and especially symbols of virtue are 'secret' or 'hidden' (1.11.36, 3.1.10, 2.8.20). We may conclude that the heroes' approaches to the 'sacred virtue[s]' pursue quests of self-discovery. Moreover, the virtues themselves, when discovered, are numinous mysteries that may even be described as 'resembling God' (5 Proem 10). In fine, the adventures go to form a greater self: to fashion a person.

At the deepest level, therefore, the poem's narrative paradigm must be discovery: the discovery that characterizes romance, rather than the conflict of epic. Of course there are many battles, and the frequency of revenge is conspicuous. But *The Faerie Queen* usually avoids any simple *enantiodromia* or war of contraries. Indeed, its most striking moral feature is reconciliation or transcendence of opposites. It pursues wholeness. Is it more anti-Papist or more

Catholic? More devoted to pleasure or to virtue? Traditional or innovative? Such questions have only to be formulated for us to see their inappropriateness. Spenser combines the great antipodes—reason and emotion, sovereignty and equity, male and female—into a single larger world of integrated identity. Not a bad emblem of *The Faerie Queen* would be Dame Concord's tempering of the fearful siblings Love and Hate (4.10.32). Unquestionably such *coincidentia oppositorum* or union of opposites runs the danger of limitless abysses. Perhaps in consequence, it arouses disagreeable apprehensions in some. Indeed, dislike of *The Faerie Queen*, when it arises, may have much to do with this feature. To lovers of the poem, distaste for it seems incomprehensibly perverse— like a distaste for life. But (again like life) *The Faerie Queen* can be difficult, dark with shades of half-thought meanings. The Victorian critics may not have been far wrong in calling it dream-like. Only, its dream analysis is more worthwhile than they cared to admit—and already expressed by Spenser in what is more alert meditation than languid fantasy.

One of the pervasive antinomies that *The Faerie Queen* attempts to combine is the one between order and change. That Spenser shared Mulcaster's and Camden's reverence for ancient tradition needs no argument. His feelings for the sanctity of civilized order finds continued and varied expression, in metaphysical celebrations, in happy ceremonies, and in praises of Queen Elizabeth, not to mention execrations of savagery and disordered licence. Nevertheless, Spenser may also be the first English poet to have written favourably of change, in any sense even remotely like what we should now call historical. In the Cantos of Mutability Nature dismisses, it is true, Dame Mutability's claim to cosmic supremacy. But she does so for a strange and subtle reason: namely, that all things indeed change, but 'by their change their being do dilate [implement]'. Mutability, which generations of poets had taken as a subject of complaint, was for Spenser something quite different: a creative process, almost a subject of encomium. Her witnesses form the grand procession of the parts of time that has offered inspiration to many subsequent poets, and that all would now concede to be a high point of his *oeuvre*. Moreover, it sums up a vision informing the entire poem, of nature in multifarious transformation.

> I well consider all that ye have said,
> And find that all things steadfastness do hate
> And changèd be: yet being rightly weighed
> They are not changèd from their first estate;
> But by their change their being do dilate:
> And turning to themselves at length again,
> Do work their own perfection so by fate:
> Then over them change doth not rule and reign;
> But they reign over change, and do their states maintain.
>
> Cease therefore daughter further to aspire,
> And thee content thus to be ruled by me:
> For thy decay thou seek'st by thy desire;
> But time shall come that all shall changèd be,
> And from thenceforth, none no more change shall see.
> So was the Titaness put down and whist [silenced],
> And Jove confirmed in his imperial see.
> Then was that whole assembly quite dismissed,
> And Nature's self did vanish, whither no man wist [knew].
>
> (7.7.58–9)

The Faerie Queen as a whole could be said to hymn creation in process, rather than created nature. It aspires to unifying change; and, by exploring far back into historical origins, ancient myths, causes of wrath, and the deepest relations of 'cousin passions', it searches, beneath outward and partial metamorphoses, for the changes of heart that could release life's fulness.

The world of *The Faerie Queen* is never vague. It may seem unsearchably vast and uncertain in measurement; but it is emotionally sure and distinctive in atmosphere. This has something to do with the long epic similes, which, like Homer's, introduce ordinary domesticities, but which have also a crisp concentrated particularity that is Spenser's own ('The watery southwind from the seaboard coast'). From time to time, too, precise sensible details come into the story itself. These would be striking but for their immediate rightness: Arthur's savage squire shook his oaken plant so

45

sternly 'That like an hazel wand, it quiverèd and quook';
Glauce 'the drunken lamp down in the oil did steep'.

In general, of course, Spenser's poem needs the unfeatured
continuum of romance. This is usually, with him, a for-
tuitous Brocéliande-like forest, 'a forest wide,/Whose hid-
eous horror and sad trembling sound/Full grisly seemed'.
This dark *verdure* serves as an unassertive background, from
which marvels stand out in highlight: a Rich Strand, perhaps, heaped with 'the wealth of the east', or a castle with
magical flames guarding its porch. But the symbolic en-
vironments themselves are as distinct as places of the mind
can well be. They are varied decisively, with a sharp dis-
crimination that will be inherited (at whatever removes) by
Dickens and Stevenson, Borges and de la Mare. One of
Spenser's forests or caves is not like another. Here the
'surges hoar,/. . . 'gainst the craggy clifts did loudly roar';
there dolphins drew the chariot of sad Cymoent so smoothly
'That their broad flaggy fins no foam did rear,/Ne bubbling
roundel they behind them sent'. (Spenser is almost always
specific about weather; being the first English, though not
the first British, poet to notice it much.) The House of
Busirane, with its grandeurs and longueurs; Malecasta's
fun house; and the difficult but desirable Temple of Venus:
these are all places we should recognize instantly. As in
dream, the presence of place is intense:

> That house's form within was rude and strong,
> Like an huge cave, hewn out of rocky clift,
> From whose rough vault the rugged breaches [fractures] hung,
> Embossed with massy gold of glorious gift,
> And with rich metal loaded every rift,
> That heavy ruin they did seem to threat;
> And over them Arachne high did lift
> Her cunning web, and spread her subtle net,
> Enwrappéd in foul smoke and clouds more black than jet.
>
> (2.7.28)

Unlike the world of common dreams, however, Spenser's
Fairyland combines emotional precision with intense lucidity.
We breathe in it a purer air that imparts not only excite-

ment to the intellect but vigour to all the faculties. Its impression is fresh; yet it has been formed by thought, long brooded, deeply meditated. Its places and landscapes are symbolic rather than allegorical in a schematic way. And if it is pondered sufficiently, it is discovered to have a profundity that justifies the stress of early criticism on Spenser's 'deep conceit'.

Such poetry has never been easy to locate on the map of Parnassus. *The Faerie Queen* contrasts, in this respect, with the work of the more fashionable Sidney, who can quite readily be related to the mannerist literary movement of his time. Spenser fits in nowhere. Neither classical nor Romantic, neither medieval nor merely neo-Gothic, neither historical nor wholly imaginary, neither fanciful nor rationally intelligible, his visionary work awaits the understanding and the judgement of ages. It has already shown an astonishing capacity to speak to our own century. How inadequate, we are bound to think (and yet how splendid too) was the inscription on Spenser's monument in Westminster Abbey naming him 'the prince of poets in his time'.

EDMUND SPENSER

A Select Bibliography

(Place of publication London, unless stated otherwise)

Bibliographies, etc.:

A REFERENCE GUIDE TO EDMUND SPENSER, by F. I. Carpenter; Chicago (1923); repr. New York (1969).

EDMUND SPENSER: A BIBLIOGRAPHICAL SUPPLEMENT, by D. F. Atkinson, Baltimore (1937); repr. New York (1967).

A CRITICAL BIBLIOGRAPHY OF THE WORKS PRINTED BEFORE 1700, by F. R. Johnson; Baltimore (1933); repr. London (1966) and Folcroft Pa. (1969).

TWO CENTURIES OF SPENSERIAN SCHOLARSHIP 1609–1805, by J. Wurtsbaugh; Baltimore (1936); repr. New York (1970), Port Washington, N.Y. (1970).

EDMUND SPENSER: AN ANNOTATED BIBLIOGRAPHY 1937–1972, by W. F. McNeir and F. Provost; Pittsburgh (1975).

CONTEMPORARY THOUGHT ON EDMUND SPENSER: WITH A BIBLIOGRAPHY OF CRITICISM OF 'THE FAERIE QUEEN', 1900–1970, ed. R. C. Frushell and B. J. Vondersmith; Carbondale, Ill., etc. (1975)

—'The Present State of Spenser Studies', by K. Williams. *Texas Studies in Language and Literature* No. 7 (1965).

A CONCORDANCE TO THE POEMS, by C. G. Osgood; Washington (1915); repr. Gloucester, Mass. (1963).

A SUBJECT-INDEX TO THE POEMS, by C. H. Whitman; New Haven (1918); repr. New York (1966).

SPENSER: THE CRITICAL HERITAGE, ed. R. M. Cummings (1971).

SPENSER NEWSLETTER. Vols. 1–5, London, Ontario (1970–74); Vols. 5– , Amherst, Mass. (1974–   ).

Collected Works:

THE FAERIE QUEEN: THE SHEPHERD'S CALENDAR: TOGETHER WITH THE OTHER WORKS OF ENGLAND'S ARCH-POET, EDM. SPENSER: COLLECTED INTO ONE VOLUME, AND CAREFULLY CORRECTED (1611 or 1617)

—the folio edns of the collected poetry; consisting of seven separate sections (independently printed at various dates, each with two main states) issued as a single volume bearing the date 1611 or 1617.

THE WORKS OF THAT FAMOUS ENGLISH POET, MR EDMUND SPENSER (1679)

—the third folio, but first collected edition of the poetry and prose, with a glossary.

THE WORKS OF MR EDMUND SPENSER, ed. J. Hughes. 6 vols. (1715)

—with a glossary and essays.

THE WORKS, ed. H. J. Todd. 8 vols. (1805)
—a variorum edition; reviewed by Walter Scott, *The Edinburgh Review* 7 (1806).
COMPLETE WORKS, ed. A. B. Grosart. 9 vols. (1882–4)
—with essays by several Victorian critics.
COMPLETE POETICAL WORKS, ed. R. E. N. Dodge; Boston (1908)
—with sparse annotation.
THE POETICAL WORKS, ed. J. C. Smith and E. de Selincourt. 3 vols. Oxford (1909–10).
—in the Oxford English Texts series, with textual and bibliographical notes.
THE POETICAL WORKS, ed. J. C. Smith and E. de Sélincourt (1912).
—the Oxford Standard Authors edition, with textual notes, a glossary and a critical Introduction by E. de Sélincourt. Contains the Spenser-Harvey letters, first printed as *Three Proper, and witty, familiar Letters*, (1580).
THE COMPLETE WORKS OF SPENSER, by W. L. Renwick. 4 vols. (1928–34)
—the incomplete Scholartis Press edn.: omits *The Faerie Queen*, but includes and annotates all the other poems. Vol. 1: *Complaints* (1928); Vol. 2: *Daphnaida and Other Poems* (1929); Vol. 3: *The Shepherd's Calendar* (1930); Vol. 4: *A View of the Present State of Ireland* (1934); repr. Oxford (1970), in modern spelling, with Index but without textual notes.
THE WORKS: A VARIORUM EDITION, ed. E. Greenlaw *et al.* 9 vols. Baltimore (1932–49); repr. with Index vol. by C. G. Osgood (1957) and *Life of Spenser* by A. C. Judson (1945), as 11 vol. set (1966).

Separate Works in Verse:

A THEATRE FOR WORLDLINGS, by S. J. van der Noodt (1569)
—containing 'Epigrams' and 'Sonnets' tr. by Spenser, rev. in *Complaints* (1591).
THE SHEPHERD'S CALENDAR. CONTAINING TWELVE ECLOGUES PROPORTIONABLE TO THE TWELVE MONTHS (1579)
—reprinted 1581, 1586, 1591, 1597; subsequently in the folio edns, and in 1653 with Latin translation. Scolar Press facs; Menston (1968).
THE FAERIE QUEEN (1590)
—Books 1–3; Letter to Raleigh. Second edn revd (1596).
THE SECOND PART OF THE FAERIE QUEEN (1596)
—Books 4–6. More copies printed than of *The Faerie Queen*, First Part (1596). Scolar facsimile of both parts of 1596 ed. G. Hough. 2 vols. (1976). Folio edn of *The Faerie Queen* (1609) is the first to include the Cantos of Mutability.

THE FAERIE QUEEN. A NEW EDITION WITH A GLOSSARY, AND NOTES
EXPLANATORY AND CRITICAL, by J. Upton. 2 vols. (1758)
—a great and classic edn.
SPENSER: THE FAERIE QUEEN, ed. A. C. Hamilton. (1977)
—in the Longman Annotated Poets series.
DAPHNAIDA. AN ELEGY UPON THE DEATH OF . . . DOUGLAS HOWARD . . .
WIFE OF ARTHUR GORGES (1591)
—reprinted with the *Hymns* (1596).
COMPLAINTS. CONTAINING SUNDRY SMALL POEMS OF THE WORLD'S
VANITY (1591)
—containing *The Ruins of Time; The Tears of the Muses; Virgil's Gnat;
Prosopopoia: or Mother Hubberd's Tale; Ruins of Rome: by Bellay;
Muiopotmos: or The Fate of the Butterfly; Visions of the World's Vanity;
The Visions of Bellay; The Visions of Petrarch.*
COLIN CLOUT'S COME HOME AGAIN (1595)
—containing the title poem; *Astrophel. A Pastoral Elegy upon the Death
of . . . Sidney* (including *The Doleful Lay of Clorinda* without a sepa-
rate title); and other elegies, one by L[odovick] B[ryskett].
AMORETTI AND EPITHALAMION (1595)
—Noel Douglas Replica (1927); Scolar Press facs. Menston (1968).
EPITHALAMION, ed. R. Beum; Columbus, Ohio (1968).
PROTHALAMION: OR: A SPOUSAL VERSE (1596).
FOUR HYMNS (1596)
—containing *An Hymn in Honour of Love; An Hymn in Honour of
Beauty; An Hymn of Heavenly Love; An Hymn of Heavenly Beauty.*
SPENSER: FOUR HYMNS: EPITHALAMION, ed. E. Welsford; Oxford (1967).

Selected Verse:

The following have useful introductions, or annotation, or both:
THE FAERIE QUEEN, BOOK 5, ed. A. B. Gough; Oxford (1918).
MAJOR BRITISH WRITERS, ed. G. B. Harrison. 2 vols; New York (1954)
—Spenser selection by C. S. Lewis, with introductory essay, 'Edmund
Spenser, 1552–99' repr. in *Studies in Medieval and Renaissance Litera-
ture*, ed. W. Hooper, Cambridge (1966).
SPENSER'S MINOR POEMS: A SELECTION, ed. R. P. C. Mutter (1957).
THE FAERIE QUEEN, BOOK 6, ed. T. A. Wolff; London and New York
(1959).
—in the Scholar's Library.
EDMUND SPENSER: SELECTED POETRY, ed. W. Nelson; New York (1964)
SPENSER: THE FAERIE QUEEN, BOOK 2, ed. P. C. Bayley; Oxford (1965).
BOOKS I AND 2 OF 'THE FAERIE QUEEN': THE MUTABILITY CANTOS AND
SELECTIONS FROM THE MINOR POETRY, ed. R. Kellogg and O. Steele;
New York (1965).

SPENSER: SELECTIONS FROM THE MINOR POEMS AND THE FAERIE QUEEN, ed. J. F. Kermode; Oxford (1965).

SPENSER: THE FAERIE QUEEN, BOOK I, ed. P. C. Bayley; Oxford (1966).

EDMUND SPENSER: SELECTED POETRY, ed. A. C. Hamilton; New York (1966)
—in the New American Library series.

EDMUND SPENSER: SELECTED POETRY, ed. L. Kirschbaum; New York (1966).

THE MUTABILITY CANTOS, ed. S. P. Zitner (1968).

EDMUND SPENSER: SELECTED POETRY, ed. A. K. and C. Hieatt; New York (1970).

EDMUND SPENSER: THE FAERIE QUEEN: A SELECTION, ed. D. Brooks-Davies (1976).

Critical and Biographical Studies:

OBSERVATIONS ON THE FAERIE QUEEN, by T. Warton (1754)
—enlarged, 2 vols. (1762); second edn repr. New York (1968), New York (1969), Farnborough (1969).

LETTERS ON CHIVALRY AND ROMANCE, by R. Hurd (1762); ed. E. J. Morley (1911); facsimile rept. of the third edn. (1765) of *Moral and Political Dialogues; with Letters on Chivalry and Romance*, 3 vols.; Farnborough (1972).

LECTURES ON THE ENGLISH POETS, by W. Hazlitt (1818).

SHAKESPEARIAN CRITICISM, by S. T. Coleridge; ed. T. M. Raysor, 2 vols. (1960). COLERIDGE'S MISCELLANEOUS CRITICISM, ed. T. M. Raysor (1936).

IMAGINATION AND FANCY, by Leigh Hunt (1844).

THE STONES OF VENICE, by J. Ruskin, vol. 2 (1853) chs. 7, 8. MODERN PAINTERS vol. 3 (1856) ch. 8.

SPENSER, by R. W. Church (1879); repr. New York (1969)
—in the English Men of Letters series.

TRANSCRIPTS AND STUDIES, by E. Dowden (1888)
—'Spenser, the Poet and Teacher', first published 1882.

THE WRITINGS OF JAMES RUSSELL LOWELL vol. 4 (1892)
—'Spenser', first published 1875.

EDMUND SPENSER: A CRITICAL STUDY, by H. E. Cory; Berkeley (1917); repr. New York (1965).

EDMUND SPENSER, by É. Legouis; Paris (1923); rev. edn. Paris (1956); English tr. (1926).

EDMUND SPENSER: AN ESSAY ON RENAISSANCE POETRY, by W. L. Renwick (1925); repr. (1965).

SPENSER IN IRELAND, by P. Henley; Cork (1928); repr. New York (1969).

VIRGIL AND SPENSER, by M. Y. Hughes; Berkeley (1929); repr. Port Washington (1969).

A SPENSER HANDBOOK, by H. S. V. Jones; New York (1930); repr. London (1947).

MYTHOLOGY AND THE RENAISSANCE TRADITION IN ENGLISH POETRY, by D. Bush; Minneapolis (1932); repr. New York (1964).

STUDIES IN SPENSER'S HISTORICAL ALLEGORY, by E. Greenlaw; Baltimore (1932); repr. New York (1967).

CLASSICAL MYTHOLOGY IN THE POETRY OF EDMUND SPENSER, by H. G. Lotspeich; Princeton (1932); repr. (1965).

SPENSER'S FAERIE QUEEN: AN INTERPRETATION, by J. Spens (1934); repr. New York (1967).

THE ALLEGORY OF LOVE, by C. S. Lewis; Oxford (1936).

THE MEANING OF SPENSER'S FAIRYLAND, by I. E. Rathborne; New York (1937); repr. New York (1965).

THE EVOLUTION OF 'THE FAERIE QUEEN', by J. W. Bennett; Chicago (1942); repr. New York (1960).

ELIZABETHAN AND METAPHYSICAL IMAGERY, by R. Tuve; Chicago (1947).

EDMUND SPENSER AND THE FAERIE QUEEN, by L. Bradner; Chicago (1948).

SHAKESPEARE, AND SPENSER by W. B. C. Watkins; Princeton (1950, 1966); repr. Cambridge, Mass. (1961).

THE RELIGIOUS BASIS OF SPENSER'S THOUGHT, by V. K. Whitaker; Stanford and London (1950); repr. Brooklyn, N.Y. (1966).

ELIZABETHAN POETRY: A STUDY IN CONVENTIONS, MEANING AND EXPRESSION, by H. Smith; Cambridge, Mass. (1952); repr. Ann Arbor, Mich. (1968).

ENGLISH LITERATURE IN THE SIXTEENTH CENTURY EXCLUDING DRAMA, by C. S. Lewis; Oxford (1954).

THE ENGLISH EPIC AND ITS BACKGROUND, by E. M. W. Tillyard; London and New York (1954).

THE ELIZABETHAN LOVE SONNET, by J. W. Lever (1956).

ON THE POETRY OF SPENSER AND THE FORM OF ROMANCES, by J. Arthos (1956); repr. New York (1970).

THE ALLEGORICAL TEMPER. VISION AND REALITY IN BOOK 2 OF SPENSER'S FAERIE QUEEN, by H. Berger. New Haven (1957); repr. Hamden (1967).

SPENSER'S CRITICS: CHANGING CURRENTS IN LITERARY TASTE, by W. R. Mueller; Syracuse, N.Y. (1959)
—selections from critics of *The Faerie Queen* from 1715–1949, with Introduction.

SHORT TIME'S ENDLESS MONUMENT. THE SYMBOLISM OF THE NUMBERS IN EDMUND SPENSER'S EPITHALAMION, by A. K. Hieatt; New York (1960); repr. Port Washington (1972).

NEOPLATONISM IN THE POETRY OF SPENSER, by R. Ellrodt; Geneva (1960)
—rev. C. S. Lewis, *Études anglaises* 14 (1961).

SPENSER, RONSARD AND DU BELLAY, by A. W. Satterthwaite; Princeton (1960).

THE STRUCTURE OF ALLEGORY IN THE FAERIE QUEEN, by A. C. Hamilton; Oxford (1961).

SPENSER'S 'SHEPHERD'S CALENDAR': A STUDY IN ELIZABETHAN ALLEGORY, by P. E. McLane. Notre Dame (1961).

THE ENDURING MOMENT: A STUDY OF THE IDEA OF PRAISE IN RENAISSANCE LITERARY THEORY AND PRACTICE, by O. B. Hardison; Chapel Hill, N.C. (1962).

A PREFACE TO THE FAERIE QUEEN, by G. Hough (1962).

THE DESCENT FROM HEAVEN: A STUDY IN EPIC CONTINUITY, by T. Greene; New Haven (1963).

FABLES OF IDENTITY: STUDIES IN POETIC MYTHOLOGY, by N. Frye; New York (1963).

THE POETRY OF EDMUND SPENSER: A STUDY, by W. Nelson; New York (1963).

THE KINDLY FLAME: A STUDY OF THE THIRD AND FOURTH BOOKS OF SPENSER'S FAERIE QUEEN, by T. P. Roche; Princeton (1964).

SPENSER AND THE NUMBERS OF TIME, by A. Fowler; London and New York (1964).

THE FIGURE OF THE POET IN RENAISSANCE EPIC, by R. Durling; Cambridge, Mass. (1965).

SPENCER'S FAERIE QUEEN: THE WORLD OF GLASS, by K. Williams; London and Berkeley (1966).

THE EARTHLY PARADISE AND THE RENAISSANCE EPIC, by A. B. Giamatti; Princeton (1966).

ALLEGORICAL IMAGERY: SOME MEDIEVAL BOOKS AND THEIR POSTERITY, by R. Tuve; Princeton (1966).

SPENSER'S IMAGES OF LIFE, by C. S. Lewis; ed. A. Fowler; Cambridge (1967).

SPENSER, by E. A. F. Watson. (1967).

THE POETRY OF THE FAERIE QUEEN, by P. J. Alpers; Princeton (1967).

SPENSER'S ALLEGORY OF JUSTICE IN BOOK FIVE OF THE FAERIE QUEEN, by T. K. Dunseath; Princeton (1968).

READING SPENSER: AN INTRODUCTION TO THE FAERIE QUEEN, by R. Sale; New York (1968).

EDMUND SPENSER'S POETRY: AUTHORITATIVE TEXTS; CRITICISM, ed. H. Maclean; New York (1968)
— texts and selections from 1590 to 1963.

EDMUND SPENSER: A CRITICAL ANTHOLOGY, ed. P. J. Alpers; Harmonds-
worth (1969)
—selections from critics from 1579 to 1968 in the Penguin paperback
edition.

A CRITICAL COMMENTARY ON SPENCER'S THE FAERIE QUEEN, by K. W.
Gransden (1969).

ICONS OF JUSTICE: ICONOGRAPHY AND THEMATIC IMAGERY IN BOOK 5 OF
THE FAERIE QUEEN, by J. Aptekar; New York (1969).

AN INTERPRETATION OF EDMUND SPENSER'S COLIN CLOUT, by S. Meyer;
Notre Dame (1969).

SPENSER'S ANATOMY OF HEROISM: A COMMENTARY ON THE FAERIE
QUEEN, by M. Evans; Cambridge (1970).

THE FAERIE QUEEN: A COMPANION FOR READERS, by R. Freeman;
London and Berkeley (1970).

THE VEIL OF ALLEGORY: SOME NOTES TOWARD A THEORY OF ALLEGORICAL
RHETORIC IN THE ENGLISH RENAISSANCE, by M. Murrin; Chicago
(1969).

EDMUND SPENSER: PRINCE OF POETS, by P. C. Bayley (1971).

THE PROPHETIC MOMENT: AN ESSAY ON SPENSER, by A. Fletcher;
Chicago and London (1971).

SOURCE AND MEANING IN SPENSER'S ALLEGORY: A STUDY OF THE FAERIE
QUEEN', by J. E. Hankins; Oxford (1971).

SPENSER'S COURTEOUS PASTORAL: BOOK SIX OF THE FAERIE QUEEN, by
H. Tonkin; Oxford (1972).

SPENSER AND LITERARY PICTORIALISM, by J. B. Bender; Princeton (1972).

THE TRANSFORMATIONS OF ALLEGORY, by G. Clifford (1974).

WELL-WEIGHED SYLLABLES: ELIZABETHAN VERSE IN CLASSICAL METRES, by
D. Attridge; Cambridge (1974).

INFERNAL TRIAD: THE FLESH, THE WORLD, AND THE DEVIL IN SPENSER AND
MILTON, by P. Cullen; Princeton (1974).

CONCEITFUL THOUGHT: THE INTERPRETATION OF ENGLISH RENAISSANCE
POEMS, by A. Fowler; Edinburgh (1975).

PLAY OF DOUBLE SENSES: SPENSER'S FAERIE QUEEN, by A. B. Giamatti;
Englewood Cliffs, N.J. (1975).

CHAUCER: SPENSER: MILTON: MYTHOPOEIC CONTINUITIES AND TRANS-
FORMATIONS, by A. K. Hieatt; Montreal and London (1975).

SPENCER'S ART. A COMPANION TO BOOK ONE OF THE FAERIE QUEEN, by
M. Rose; Cambridge, Mass. (1975).

ASTRAEA: THE IMPERIAL THEME IN THE SIXTEENTH CENTURY, by F. A.
Yates (1975).

SPENSER'S ALLEGORY: THE ANATOMY OF IMAGINATION, by I. G. Mac-
Caffrey; Princeton (1976).

THE ANALOGY OF THE FAERIE QUEEN, by J. Nohrnberg; Princeton (1976).
SPENCER'S FAERIE QUEEN: A CRITICAL COMMENTARY ON BOOKS 1 and 2, by D. Brooks-Davies, Manchester (1977).

Some Articles:

Note: contains only a few articles of historical importance or special interest to the compiler. Necessarily omits many papers of importance, and all those collected in books already listed.

'Spenser's Garden of Adonis', by J. W. Bennett. *PMLA* 47 (1932).

'Elizabeth as Astraea', by F. A. Yates. *Journal of the Warburg and Courtauld Inst.* 10 (1947).

'The Argument of Spenser's *Shepherd's Calendar*', by A. C. Hamilton. *Journal of English Literary History* 23 (1956).

'Spenser's Calendar of Christian Time', by R. A. Durr. *Journal of English Literary History* 24 (1957).

'Una and the Clergy; the Ass Symbol in *The Faerie Queen*', by J. M. Steadman. *Journal of the Warburg and Courtauld Inst.* 21 (1958).

'Nature and Grace in *The Faerie Queen:* The Problem Reviewed', by T. M. Gang. *Journal of English Literary History* 26 (1959).

IMAGE AND MEANING: METAPHORIC TRADITIONS IN RENAISSANCE POETRY, by D. C. Allen. Baltimore (1960); rev. edn. (1968)

—'The March Eclogue of *The Shepherd's Calendar*' and '*Muiopotmos*'.

ELIZABETHAN POETRY, ed. J. R. Brown and B. Harris (1960)

—'No Room at the Top: Spenser's Pursuit of Fame' by M. C. Bradbrook.

FORM AND CONVENTION IN THE POETRY OF EDMUND SPENSER, ed. W. Nelson. Selected Papers from the English Inst. Columbia Univ. New York and London (1961).

'Platonic Allegory in *The Faerie Queen*', by M. Evans. *Review of English Studies* 12 (1961).

'Some Themes in Spenser's *Prothalamion*', by D. H. Woodward. *Journal of English Literary History* 29 (1962).

'The Implications of Form for *The Shepherd's Calendar*', by S. K. Heninger. *Studies in the Renaissance* 9 (1962).

'Elizabethan Architecture and *The Faerie Queen:* Some Structural Analogies', by J. Dundas. *Dalhousie Review* 45 (1966).

'Spenser's Diction and Classical Precedent', by S. P. Zitner. *Philological Quarterly* 45 (1966).

'Giants and Tyrants in Book Five of *The Faerie Queen*', by R. O. Iredale. *Review of English Studies* 17 (1966).

PATTERNS OF LOVE AND COURTESY: ESSAYS IN MEMORY OF C. S. LEWIS, ed. J. Lawlor. Evanston, Ill. (1966)

—'Order, Grace and Courtesy in Spenser's World', by P. C. Bayley.

'Edmund Spenser: An Introductory Essay', by M. MacLure. *Queen's Quarterly* 73 (1966).

LITERARY CRITICISM AND HISTORICAL UNDERSTANDING, ed. P. Damon. Selected Papers from the English Institute. New York and London (1967).

—'Autobiography and Art: An Elizabethan Borderland', by R. B. Gottfried.

THAT SOVEREIGN LIGHT. ESSAYS IN HONOUR OF EDMUND SPENSER, 1552–1952, ed. W. R. Mueller and D. C. Allen; Baltimore (1952); repr. New York (1967).

'Spenser's *Epithalamion*: The Harmonious Universe of Love', by A. R. Cirillo. *Studies in English Literature 1500–1900* 8 (1968).

'The Rhetorical Basis of Spenser's Imagery', by J. Dundas; *Studies in English Literature 1500–1900* 8 (1968).

THE PRINCE OF POETS: ESSAYS ON EDMUND SPENSER, ed. R. R. Elliott. New York (1968).

'Our New Poet: Archetypal Criticism and *The Faerie Queen*', by R. B. Gottfried. *PMLA* 83 (1968).

'Spenser and the Common Reader', by A. C. Hamilton. *Journal of English Literary History* 35 (1968).

'Structure and Ceremony in Spenser's *Epithalamion*', by M. A. Wickert. *Journal of English Literary History* 35 (1968).

SPENSER: A COLLECTION OF CRITICAL ESSAYS, ed. H. Berger; Englewood Cliffs, N.J. (1968).

'*The Shepherd's Calendar*—a Structural Analysis', by M. S. Røstvig. *Renaissance and Medieval Studies* 13 (1969).

'An Iconographical Puzzle: Spenser's Cupid at *Faerie Queen* 2.8', by R. M. Cummings. *Journal of the Warburg and Courtauld Inst.* 33 (1970).

SILENT POETRY: ESSAYS IN NUMEROLOGICAL ANALYSIS, ed. A. Fowler; London and New York (1970).

—'Placement "in the middest", in *The Faerie Queen*', by M. Baybak *et al.* and 'The Unity of Spenser's *Amoretti*', by A. Dunlop.

'Spenser's Sonnet Diction', by W. C. Johnson. *Neuphilologische Mitteilungen* 71 (1970).

ENGLISH POETRY AND PROSE, 1540–1674, ed. C. B. Ricks (1970)
—includes 'Spenser' by M. MacLure.

CRITICAL ESSAYS ON SPENSER FROM *ELH*, ed. Editors of the *Journal of English Literary History*; Baltimore (1970).

'Busirane and the War Between the Sexes: An Interpretation of *The Faerie Queen*, 3.11–12', by H. Berger. *English Literary Renaissance* 1 (1971).

56

'Spenser and the Mingled Measure', by J. Hollander. *English Literary Renaissance* 1 (1971).

SHAKESPEARE, SPENSER, DONNE: RENAISSANCE ESSAYS, by J. F. Kermode; London and New York (1971).

'ETERNE IN MUTABILITY': THE UNITY OF THE FAERIE QUEEN: ESSAYS PUBLISHED IN MEMORY OF DAVID PHILOON HARDING 1914–1970, ed. K. J. Atchity; Hamden, Conn. (1972).

ESSENTIAL ARTICLES FOR THE STUDY OF EDMUND SPENSER, ed. A. C. Hamilton, Hamden, Conn. (1972).

'Order and Joy in Spenser's *Epithalamion*', by W. S. Hill. *Southern Humanities Review* 6 (1972).

'Amor and Spenser's *Amoretti*', by W. C. Johnson. *English Studies* 51 (1973).

A THEATRE FOR SPENSERIANS: PAPERS OF THE INTERNATIONAL SPENSER COLLOQUIUM, FREDERICTON 1969, ed. J. M. Kennedy and J. A. Reither; Toronto (1973).

FIRST IMAGES OF AMERICA: THE IMPACT OF THE NEW WORLD ON THE OLD, ed. F. Chiappelli *et al*, etc. Berkeley (1976)
—'Primitivism and the Process of Civility in Spenser's *Faerie Queen*' by A. B. Giamatti.

'Spenser and the Renaissance Mythology of Love', by W. V. Nestrick; *Literary Monographs* 6, ed. E. Rothstein and J. A. Wittreich. Madison, Wisc. (1975).

SPENSER: THE FAERIE QUEEN, ed. P. C Bayley (1977)
—in the Casebook Series.

WRITERS AND THEIR WORK

General Surveys:
THE DETECTIVE STORY IN BRITAIN:
Julian Symons
THE ENGLISH BIBLE: Donald Coggan
ENGLISH MARITIME WRITING:
Hakluyt to Cook: Oliver Warner
ENGLISH SERMONS: Arthur Pollard
THE ENGLISH SHORT STORY I: & II:
T. O. Beachcroft
THE ENGLISH SONNET: P. Cruttwell
ENGLISH TRANSLATORS AND
TRANSLATIONS: J. M. Cohen
ENGLISH TRAVELLERS IN THE
NEAR EAST: Robin Fedden

Sixteenth Century and Earlier:
BACON: J. Max Patrick
BEAUMONT & FLETCHER: Ian Fletcher
CHAUCER: Nevill Coghill
GOWER & LYDGATE: Derek Pearsall
HOOKER: Arthur Pollard
KYD: Philip Edwards
LANGLAND: Nevill Coghill
LYLY & PEELE: G. K. Hunter
MALORY: M. C. Bradbrook
MARLOWE: Philip Henderson
MORE: E. E. Reynolds
RALEGH: Agnes Latham
SIDNEY: Kenneth Muir
SKELTON: Peter Green
SPENSER: Rosemary Freeman
TWO SCOTS CHAUCERIANS:
H. Harvey Wood
WYATT: Sergio Baldi

Seventeenth Century:
BROWNE: Peter Green
BUNYAN: Henri Talon
CAVALIER POETS: Robin Skelton
CONGREVE: Bonamy Dobrée
DONNE: J. F. Kermode
DRYDEN: Bonamy Dobrée
ENGLISH DIARISTS:
Evelyn and Pepys: M. Willy
FARQUHAR: A. J. Farmer
JOHN FORD: Clifford Leech

HERBERT: T. S. Eliot
HERRICK: John Press
HOBBES: T. E. Jessop
BEN JONSON: J. B. Bamborough
LOCKE: Maurice Cranston
MARVELL: John Press
MILTON: E. M. W. Tillyard
RESTORATION COURT POETS:
V. de S. Pinto
SHAKESPEARE: C. J. Sisson
CHRONICLES: Clifford Leech
EARLY COMEDIES: Derek Traversi
LATER COMEDIES: G. K. Hunter
FINAL PLAYS: J. F. Kermode
HISTORIES: L. C. Knights
POEMS: F. T. Prince
PROBLEM PLAYS: Peter Ure
ROMAN PLAYS: T. J. B. Spencer
GREAT TRAGEDIES: Kenneth Muir
THREE METAPHYSICAL POETS:
Margaret Willy
WALTON: Margaret Bottrall
WEBSTER: Ian Scott-Kilvert
WYCHERLEY: P. F. Vernon

Eighteenth Century:
BERKELEY: T. E. Jessop
BLAKE: Kathleen Raine
BOSWELL: P. A. W. Collins
BURKE: T. E. Utley
BURNS: David Daiches
WM COLLINS: Oswald Doughty
COWPER: N. Nicholson
CRABBE: R. L. Brett
DEFOE: J. R. Sutherland
FIELDING: John Butt
GAY: Oliver Warner
GIBBON: C. V. Wedgwood
GOLDSMITH: A. Norman Jeffares
GRAY: R. W. Ketton-Cremer
HUME: Montgomery Belgion
SAMUEL JOHNSON: S. C. Roberts
POPE: Ian Jack
RICHARDSON: R. F. Brissenden
SHERIDAN: W. A. Darlington
SMART: Geoffrey Grigson

SMOLLETT: Laurence Brander
STEELE, ADDISON: A. R. Humphreys
STERNE: D. W. Jefferson
SWIFT: J. Middleton Murry (1955)
SWIFT: A. Norman Jeffares (1976)
VANBRUGH: Bernard Harris
HORACE WALPOLE: Hugh Honour

Nineteenth Century:
ARNOLD: Kenneth Allott
AUSTEN: S. Townsend Warner (1951)
AUSTEN: B. C. Southam (1975)
BAGEHOT: N. St John-Stevas
THE BRONTË SISTERS:
                Phyllis Bentley (1950)
THE BRONTËS: I & II: Winifred Gérin
E. B. BROWNING: Alethea Hayter
ROBERT BROWNING: John Bryson
SAMUEL BUTLER: G. D. H. Cole
BYRON: I, II & III: Bernard Blackstone
CARLYLE: David Gascoyne
CARROLL: Derek Hudson
CLOUGH: Isobel Armstrong
COLERIDGE: Kathleen Raine
CREEVEY & GREVILLE: J. Richardson
DE QUINCEY: Hugh Sykes Davies
DICKENS: K. J. Fielding
    EARLY NOVELS: T. Blount
    LATER NOVELS: B. Hardy
DISRAELI: Paul Bloomfield
GEORGE ELIOT: Lettice Cooper
FITZGERALD: Joanna Richardson
GASKELL: Miriam Allott
GISSING: A. C. Ward
HARDY: R. A. Scott-James
                and C. Day Lewis
HAZLITT: J. B. Priestley (1960)
HAZLITT: R. L. Brett (1977)
HOOD: Laurence Brander
HOPKINS: Geoffrey Grigson
T. H. HUXLEY: William Irvine
KEATS: Edmund Blunden (1950)
KEATS: Miriam Allott (1976)
LAMB: Edmund Blunden
LANDOR: G. Rostrevor Hamilton
LEAR: Joanna Richardson
MACAULAY: G. R. Potter (1959)
MACAULAY: Kenneth Young (1976)

MEREDITH: Phyllis Bartlett
MILL: Maurice Cranston
MORRIS: P. Henderson
NEWMAN: J. M. Cameron
PATER: Ian Fletcher
PEACOCK: J. I. M. Stewart
CHRISTINA ROSSETTI: G. Battiscombe
D. G. ROSSETTI: Oswald Doughty
RUSKIN: Peter Quennell
SCOTT: Ian Jack
SHELLEY: G. M. Matthews
SOUTHEY: Geoffrey Carnall
STEPHEN: Phyllis Grosskurth
STEVENSON: G. B. Stern
SWINBURNE: Ian Fletcher
TENNYSON: B. C. Southam
THACKERAY: Laurence Brander
FRANCIS THOMPSON: P. Butter
TROLLOPE: Hugh Sykes Davies
WILDE: James Laver
WORDSWORTH: Helen Darbishire

Twentieth Century:
ACHEBE: A. Ravenscroft
ARDEN: Glenda Leeming
AUDEN: Richard Hoggart
BECKETT: J-J. Mayoux
BENNETT: Frank Swinnerton (1950)
BENNETT: Kenneth Young (1975)
BETJEMAN: John Press
BLUNDEN: Alec M. Hardie
BOND: Simon Trussler
BRIDGES: J. Sparrow
BURGESS: Carol M. Dix
CAMPBELL: David Wright
CARY: Walter Allen
CHESTERTON: C. Hollis
CHURCHILL: John Connell
COLLINGWOOD: E. W. F. Tomlin
COMPTON-BURNETT: R. Glynn Grylls
CONRAD: Oliver Warner (1950)
CONRAD: C. B. Cox (1977)
DE LA MARE: Kenneth Hopkins
NORMAN DOUGLAS: Ian Greenlees
LAWRENCE DURRELL: G. S. Fraser
T. S. ELIOT: M. C. Bradbrook
T. S. ELIOT: The Making of
'The Waste Land': M. C. Bradbrook